Praise for the book

In this era where inequality, economic and ecological indifferences are widespread, and have indeed become the norm, we must search for another way of organizing collective existence. That is what *Living in Truth* tries to articulate. The book's focus is Gandhi, but it offers an alternative vision of living and being together. The authors consider various detritus of the contemporary world, all of which they contend are linked to an ethical deficiency or myopia to which Gandhi had an alternative. This book's message is very timely and important, both to scholars and to ordinary citizens. It should be widely read.

—**Uday Singh Mehta,**
Professor of political philosophy,
Center of City University, New York

This book is an extremely valuable contribution to the Gandhian mode of philosophical thinking. The world today is riven with serious political, social, economic and ecological crises. Large parts of the developing world continue to be abysmally poor. Significant and growing economic inequalities are features of both rich and poor countries, and are usually the necessary concomitants of the capitalistic growth process. Several countries are in the midst of dangerous military conflagrations. The very survival of the planet seems to be at stake.

Is there any chance of redressal? It is possible to hold the view that Gandhiji's ethical approach, based fundamentally on truth, non-violence and the Socratic moral idea of self-examination, offers much hope. Ironically, while there appears to be keen interest across the world regarding the Gandhian mode, within India, its reconsideration seems to be less than enthusiastic. The authors of this book explore several crucial dimensions of the Gandhian paradigm. The reader of this slim volume is assured of a rich fare.

—**Pulin Nayak,**
Former Director and Professor, Delhi School of Economics

LIVING *in* TRUTH

LIVING *in* TRUTH

THE GANDHIAN PARADIGM

Ramin Jahanbegloo *and* Pooja Sharma

RUPA

Published by
Rupa Publications India Pvt. Ltd 2022
7/16, Ansari Road, Daryaganj
New Delhi 110002

Sales centres:
Allahabad Bengaluru Chennai
Hyderabad Jaipur Kathmandu
Kolkata Mumbai

ISBN: 978-93-5520-782-1

First impression 2022

10 9 8 7 6 5 4 3 2 1

Printed in India

Contents

Introduction

It is our aim in the following pages to give a full and rounded picture of Mahatma Gandhi's relevance to our world, both in its ethical-political and economic-ecological aspects. Gandhi's life and contributions have been the subjects of countless books and essays, but rarely have his thoughts and actions been approached and analysed in terms of a paradigm. Many, if not most, people have probably never heard of the concept of paradigm. The word comes from the Greek term, παράδειγμα (*paradeigma*), which means pattern or example. A paradigm is thus a guiding idea or a conceptual framework.

As such, when we speak of 'Gandhi's paradigm', we refer to the exemplarity of his thoughts and actions, which we can say, touched every aspect of Indian ethical, political and economic life. His leadership was paradigmatic and became one with the life of the Indian nation. However, we can also add that the Gandhian paradigm has a universal value in today's world, because it provides a model solution to a great number of our global challenges. The Gandhian paradigm, in its initial form that was developed in Gandhi's seminal work, *Hind Swaraj* (1909), and its contemporary analysis, have had an impact on our mode of thinking about the two concepts of tradition and modernity. But, it has also changed the way we think about humankind's spiritual and rational attempts at understanding the world. Before Gandhi, our views on politics and economics were dominated by a heroic narrative of technoscientific progress. Gandhi did not try to add a new truth to the existing stock of old truths. In their book, Llyod I. Rudolph and Susanne Hoeber Rudolph had said:

> Gandhi's epistemology was rooted in 'truth in action', a concept that locates truth in the facts and circumstance of particular situation... For Gandhi, truth had several meanings and forms. It could be situational as in the goal of a satyagraha, contextual and contingent as in the experimental truths found in his autobiography, and absolute as in his commitment to 'Truth in God'.[1]

Gandhi usually spoke of truth in terms of self-experience, rather than universal cognition. 'Truth,' he said, 'resides in every human heart, and one has to search for it there, and to be guided by truth as one sees it. But no one has the right to coerce others to act according to his own view of truth.'[2] Gandhi considered the search for truth an integral part of his non-violence and a vital component of the relationship between the private and the public. Dennis Dalton, a political science professor, said:

> The point of achieving individual self-realization as a vital component of the political method of satyagraha

[1]Rudolph, Llyod I., and Susanne Hoeber Rudolph, *Postmodern Gandhi and Other Essays: Gandhi in the World and at Home*, The University of Chicago Press, Chicago, 2006, pp. 5–7.

[2]Attri, Rajinder, Dr, *Gandhian Thoughts*, Sarla Publications, Shimla, 2018, p. 99.

> is related to Gandhi's vision of the ultimate source of conflict resolution. He contended that the seeming diversity of individual interests could be ultimately reconciled in terms of a higher unity or consensus. The unity was expressed in a religious ethic of spiritual oneness.[3]

The main point here is the difference between the possession of a final truth and the permanent search of an experimental truth as a common ground for non-violence.

Briefly put, in this book, we are of the view that the essence of the Gandhian paradigm is the effort of searching for meaning in a meaningless world. His going beyond (para-) the everydayness to show (*deiknynai*) the relationship between the ideal and the real was a way of raising the ethical aspiration of the citizens and the non-violent essence of the government. What set Gandhi apart was his belief in transformative leadership and citizenry. 'Gandhi's particular accomplishment as a political leader was to relate both the power of sataygraha and the purpose of swaraj to the ideal of inclusivity... Gandhi saw the task of leadership as educative in another sense, that satyagraha must be used to gain the empowerment of those who had never been politicized.'[4] If Gandhi's critique of the political has any relevance today, it is due to two main factors: on the one hand, contemporary politics lacks moral leaders, and on the other hand, democracies around world have abandoned

---

[3]Dalton, Dennis, *Mahatma Gandhi: Nonviolent Power in Action*, Columbia University Press, New York, 1993, p. 44.
[4]Ibid. 193–4.

the empowerment of the weakest in favour of economic and political supremacy, and hegemony of the strongest. However, Gandhi's view of democracy was exactly the opposite. 'My notion of democracy,' he observed, 'is that under it the weakest should have the same opportunity as the strongest. That can never happen except through non-violence.'[5] The Gandhian paradigm is, therefore, based on truthfulness and non-violence. However, as we will see throughout this book, Gandhi also established an essential relationship between social awareness and common humanity. For him, politics as the art of organizing society was a path to self-realization and autonomy of the individual and the community.

The truth is that the Gandhian revolution was not only political, but also ethical and spiritual. Gandhi not only spiritualized Indian politics by making it truthful and exemplary but also brought about ethicality in Indian economy by opting for a network of mutuality and solidarity. A thorough reading of Gandhi's 100 volumes of *Collected Works* reveals no ambiguity. Gandhi's distinctive quality was not merely his love of equality, inclusivity and the spiritual equilibrium between humankind and other living creatures but also his exemplary persistence on respect of the other. He argued: 'Earth provides enough to satisfy every man's need but not every man's greed.'[6] This vision continues to hold political contemporaneity and spiritual

---

[5]Kripalani, Krishna (ed.), *All Men are Brothers: Life and Thoughts of Mahatma Gandhi As Told in His* Own Words, Navajivan Publishing House, Ahmedabad, 1960, p. 177.

[6]Pandey, Janardan (ed.), *Gandhi and 21st Century*, Concept Publishing Company, New Delhi, 1998, p. 142.

power because it grew out of the process of incubation and intellectual maturation of the Gandhian paradigm. Assuredly, a variety of intellectual ruptures and spiritual experiments operated together throughout to develop Gandhi's life in his triple vision of swaraj, satyagraha and sarvodaya. Swaraj and satyagraha are the two mother concepts of Gandhian social and political philosophy. At the heart of the Gandhian doctrine of self-emancipation and self-determination, we find the concept of swaraj. As a point of connection between ethics and politics, swaraj incorporated many other aspects of the Gandhian thought, including trusteeship. At the centre of this concept was the urge to promote equity and justice, while reducing the gap between the rich and the poor to a minimum. Accordingly, Gandhi believed that 'economics is untrue which ignores or disregards moral values. The extension of the law of non-violence in the domain of economics means nothing less than the introduction of moral values as a factor to be considered in regulating international commerce.'[7] As such, far from having a utopian vision of the economic order, Gandhi believed in equal partnership of entrepreneurs, workers and consumers. However, more than just being a methodology, Gandhian trusteeship is a way of life. As Gandhi argued:

> The real implication of equal distribution is that each man shall have the wherewithal to supply all his natural wants and no more. For example, if one man has a

---

[7]Kripalani, Krishna (ed.), *All Men are Brothers: Life and Thoughts of Mahatma Gandhi As Told in His Own Words*, Navajivan Publishing House, Ahmedabad, 1960, p. 166.

> weak digestion and requires only a quarter of a pound of flour for his bread and another needs a pound, both should be in a position to satisfy their wants. To bring this ideal into being the entire social order has got to be reconstructed. A society based on non-violence cannot nurture any other ideal. We may not perhaps be able to realize the goal but we must bear it in mind and work unceasingly to near it. To the same extent as we progress towards our goal we shall find contentment and happiness, and to that extent too, shall we have contributed towards the bringing into being of a non-violent society.[8]

It goes without saying that the Gandhian revolution was integral because it took into account not only the domains of the ethical and the political but also established a new anthropology. Gandhi believed, 'All men are brothers and no human being should be a stranger to another. The welfare of all, sarvodaya, should be our aim. God is the common bond that unites all human beings. To break this bond even with our greatest enemy is to tear God Himself to pieces. There is humanity even in the most wicked.'[9] We can fully understand hereby the inclusive character of the Gandhian model of interconnectedness. As we can see, Gandhi's innovation emerges in relation to the development of Indian concepts, like swaraj, satyagraha and sarvodaya, in a global context. Thus, Gandhi extended his ideal of swaraj to the capacity for self-rule, birth of truth and

---

[8]Ibid. 169.

[9]Ibid. viii.

non-violence, all being directed towards the upliftment of all categories of citizens. As a result, Gandhian political anthropology was founded on the argument that the belief that 'there is no connection between the means and the end is a great mistake'.[10] The consequence that Gandhi drew from this convertibility between means and ends was that no individual or community could have the pretension to understand humanity and the world without encouraging the pursuit of truth and embracing all forms of non-violent action. In this respect, it's certainly regrettable that Gandhi's serious commitment to non-violence and welfare of all has not been taken seriously by many political and corporate leaders around the world.

Undoubtedly, Gandhi's alternatives to the political and economic ills of our world can bring back the truthful force of spirituality, and the ethical needs of humankind to the forefront of our global struggles, like climate change, poverty, rise of populism, influx of refugees and the domination of the world economy by the corporate mindset. That is why, these days, the Gandhi-esque slogans, such as 'simple living' and 'small is beautiful', seem suited to the needs and ideals of the twenty-first century. The Gandhian paradigm of 'living in truth', which Václav Havel referred to as a mode of resistance in an ideological state, was a strategy that fostered empathy and compassion.[11] Unsurprisingly, all the inheritors of Gandhi, like Martin Luther King Jr, Nelson Mandela, Havel, His Holiness the Dalai Lama, etc., well understood what

[10]Ibid. 107.

[11]Havel, Václav, *Open Letters: Selected Writings 1965-1990*, Vintage Books, New York, 1992, pp. 196–8.

Gandhi meant by the hidden powers of the soul. And yet, Gandhi's own approach was the most interesting. He said:

> I am engaged in trying to show, if I have any of these powers, that I am as frail a mortal as any of us and that I never had anything extraordinary about me nor have any now. I claim to be a simple individual liable to err like any other fellow mortal. I own, however, that I have humility enough to confess my errors and to retrace my steps.[12]

Gandhi knew well that empathy, solidarity and interconnectedness were the keys to the prioritization of social justice, equity, harmony and non-violence in our world. What he suggested, therefore, was to develop a humanitarian pedagogy against greed, self-centredness, arrogance and brutality. Moreover, Gandhi's pedagogy for harmonious exchange and living democracy underlined the necessity for a new ecological vision. For Gandhi, the spiritualization of the modern economic mindset basically meant to transcend the tragic separation of the humankind from nature. Questioning the moral irresponsibility of the techno-capitalist civilization, Gandhi said that the modern project of 'conquest' and 'domination' of Earth is a mortal danger to the natural biodiversity and all the indigenous cultures. The Gandhian revolution, as developed in *Hind Swaraj*, represents an ethical and political challenge to the reductionist essence of the concept of 'progress'.

[12]Gandhi, M.K., *The Essential Gandhi: An Anthology of His Writings on His Life, Work, and Ideas*, Louis Fischer (ed.), Vintage Books, New York, 1962, pp. 179–80.

Consequently, the Gandhian paradigm is the recognition and the transformation of the conquest of nature and human beings through the idea of progress. The Gandhian project of love and care for the 'otherness of the other' went hand in hand with a new gaze on the definition of rationality, and its economic and ecological expressions. Thus, with Gandhi, we have a revolutionary who not only changed the Cartesian view on human nature but also emphasized on a shared meaning of life between humans and non-humans. In fact, Gandhi deeply believed that peace with the world would not be possible till human beings transcend their selfish interests. For Gandhi, empathy and compassion were not cultural choices, but values that combined interconnectedness and spiritual growth of humanity.

At the same time, Gandhi considered himself as a practical idealist, who combined his 'experiments with truth' and a high moral attitude towards the 'otherness of the other'. For Gandhi, life was not a matter of 'spiritual knowledge', but that of 'spiritual growth'. He underlined: 'We often confuse spiritual knowledge with spiritual attainment. Spirituality is not a matter of knowing scriptures and engaging in philosophical discussions. It is a matter of heart culture, of unmeasurable strength. Fearlessness is the first requisite of spirituality. Cowards can never be moral.'[13]

Let us be clear: the Gandhian paradigm is a spiritual project of change and transformation of humanity in its relation with the world. Gandhi was convinced that

---

[13]Kripalani, Krishna (ed.), *All Men are Brothers: Life and Thoughts of Mahatma Gandhi As Told in His Own Words*, Navajivan Publishing House, Ahmedabad, 1960, p. 102.

'a civilization which makes the attainment of material pleasures as one of the central objects of life and sanctions extreme violence against nature, non-human life-forms and sections of humanity for achieving material ends is not a civilization which can be conducive for the upholding of higher ethical principles'.[14] All through out his life, Gandhi kept his moral commitment to the *ahimsic* (non-violent and harmless) nursing and healing of humans and non-humans. His sensibilities towards the disastrous effects of unchecked modernization and unbridled progress were completed by his efforts to fight against the environmental degradation of Indian biodiversity and individual moral corruption. As such, Gandhian paradigm was coherent with his life, since he followed his moral and spiritual commitments until the very end. He gave priority to the frail and the fragile by struggling for the weakest and the poorest in the public sphere. He also stood firmly on Mother Earth's side, fighting the proliferation of unlimited economic and technological growth.

Thus, at the centre of Gandhi's philosophy of life, we can find the idea of need against greed and the condemnation of a civilization with no self-control. That is why, Gandhi was ahead of his time in criticizing and disapproving the growing menace of ecological degradation, consumerism and mechanization social life. The challenges of the twenty-first century gives us an opportunity to go back to Mahatma Gandhi and to rethink about different facets of our

---

[14]Jain, Satish K., 'On Hind Swaraj Discourse on Institutions and Technology', *Reflections on Hind Swaraj*, Siby K. Joseph and Bharat Mahodaya (eds.), Institute of Gandhian Studies, Wardha, 2011, p. 49.

world in the mirror of the Gandhian paradigm.

Gandhi's commitment to ethical and moral revolution could be visualized in his notion of economics. Emerging from the primary dimension of upliftment and enrichment of human life, the fundamentals of Gandhian economics measure economic welfare and growth not as materialistic pleasure but value the extent of ultimate satisfaction that is followed by spiritual enlightenment. The law of non-possession forms the basis of the entire philosophy of the Gandhian economic revolution.

The economic growth led by human civilization has been the primary cause of unprecedented consumerism. As a result, humans have been trapped in the vicious cycle of unlimited wants. Greed, competition, vested interest and preponderance of power have become the basic nature of humankind. Equity and distribution have been conveniently ignored under such an economic framework. In contrast, the Gandhian trusteeship model becomes a means to transform the present capitalist order of the society into an egalitarian one. It gives no quarter to capitalism but gives the present owning class a chance to reform itself. It is based on the faith that human nature is never beyond redemption.[15]

Gandhian economics revolves around the ethical revolution of humans who can morally distinguish between desire and need. The inner voice, which makes this ethical judgement, as suggested by Gandhi, was to some extent similar to 'an impartial spectator' suggested by Adam Smith, the 'father of modern economics'. Nicholas Phillipson

[15]Gandhi, M.K., *Trusteeship*, Ravindra Kelkar (ed.), Navajivan Publishing House, Ahmedabad, 1960.

equated Smith's use of the term 'impartial spectator' with the voice of conscience or even that of the deity as both are judgemental.[16]

Gandhian economics stands distinct from the classical school of thought proposed by Smith where markets achieve equilibrium with the help of 'invisible hands'. In Gandhian economics, the ethical pursuit of humans is the guiding force for achieving sustainable economic growth. The classical theory of invisible hands was criticized by Marxian economics by advocating the labour theory of value. But Gandhian economics deviates from Marxists' notion of economics based on the fundamental principle of materialism. Though both the theories were focused on achieving equality and justice, primarily reflecting similar ends, the means deployed were distinct. Marx adopted revolution by uniting the labour force against injustice, while Gandhi called for an ethical and moral revolution.

Eventually, the neoclassical-Keynesian school of thought emerged post Second World War, advocating the role of government. The Keynesian belief that the increasing demand could lead to a multiplier effect and would be equally distributed to the poor also fell apart. This was from the experience of the stagflation during the 1970s.[17] Gandhian economics provides an alternate view and revolutionizes the fundamentals of economics, fortifying that material wants should not be the key driver of economic growth. The ethical aim of every economic system must be to attain happiness,

---

[16]Phillipson, Nicholas, *Adam Smith: An Enlightened Life*, Penguin, UK, 2010.

[17]Skidelsky, Robert, *Keynes: The Return of the Master*, Penguin, UK, 2010.

sociological and psychological well-being, and ultimately, sustain human dignity.

India's Intended Nationally Determined Contributions is based on the Gandhian notion of trusteeship. Gandhi had said that we should act as 'trustees' and use natural resources wisely, as it is our moral responsibility to ensure that we bequeath to the future generations a healthy planet.[18] Gandhian trusteeship concept is a remarkable breakthrough in the fundamentals of economics, unfolding the problem of scarcity by proposing the most efficient way of treating surplus. Trusteeship doctrine emerges from the law of non-possession, where possessing material things is considered theft.

Gandhi contended:

> The rich people who have accumulated excessive wealth should distribute it for maximising the welfare of the rest of the community. The wealth belongs to the entire community. Wealthy people should consider themselves to be the trustees. However, no force should be used to acquire their wealth. Their wealth should be used properly through their consent as trustees.[19]

The core of trusteeship is the protection of human dignity and not merely material prosperity. Wealth should be

---

[18]'India's Climate Change Commitment Based on Gandhian Principles', *Business Line*, 22 January 2018, https://bit.ly/3ICeVve. Accessed on 14 July 2022.

[19]Ghosh, B.N., *Gandhian Political Economy: Principles, Practice and Policy (Alternative Voices in Contemporary Economics)*, Ashgate Publishing, 2007, p. 16.

distributed to bring equality of ownership of income, narrowing the class gap.[20]

According to the Gandhian principles of economics, the rules of the game are not 'invisible hands' operating in the market as suggested by Smith but fundamentals guided by the soul force, based on ethical and moral evolution of self. In such an economy, welfare is defined as the ultimate satisfaction of every entity, ensuring a Pareto optimality, a state wherein everyone attains satisfaction. Thus, the Gandhian economic revolution departs from Marxist economics, as it is intensely spiritual. On the other hand, Marxist economics is confined to material equity and market mechanism requiring government intervention.

Gandhian economics attains self-sufficiency and self-satisfaction by advocating a decentralized setting, wherein the economic agent is spiritually and ethically evolved and manifests the absolute truth. The objective of this economic system is to maximize both material and spiritual utility based on needs and not wants or desires. Thus, the whole fundamentals of Gandhian economics differ from both classical and Keynesian economics. While the latter justifies the role of government to attain full employment, Gandhian economics advocates the role of government for maintaining law and order along with the health, social security and welfare of the people. The decentralized systems across regions, based on consensus, will deliver a more egalitarian, peaceful and non-violent society.

[20]*Gandhi Marg*, Vol. 25, No. 4, 2004.

The Gandhian ethical and moral connection was not only limited to humankind but also extended to non-human entities in nature. The connection between humans and nature, as perceived by Gandhi, was not simply materialistic, but was interconnectedness at a spiritual level. This spiritual connection, he said, could be envisaged only by realizing the absolute truth that manifests out of absolute love for every human and non-human entity in the environment. Gandhi contended, 'Nature suffices for my inspiration.'[21] He believed in universal coexistence and considered non-violence as a universal law of life, which manifests in love for all creatures.

Human beings have been caught up in the vicious cycle of consumerism. The fallout of unchecked consumerism is primarily evident in the most severe global challenge of climate change. The world has begun to realize the challenge of 'meeting the needs of the present generation without compromising the ability of future generations to meet their needs'.[22] Sustainable Development Goals (SDGs) were born at the United Nations Conference on Sustainable Development in Rio de Janeiro in 2012.[23] Later in the mid of 2000, Environmental Social Governance (ESG) reinforced the need for conscious and shared responsibility to the

---

[21]Chatterjee, Margaret, *Gandhi's Religious Thought,* Macmillan, London, 1983, p. 65.

[22]*Report of the World Commission on Environment and Development: Our Common Future,* United Nations, 1987.

[23]'United Nations Conference on Sustainable Development, Rio+20', Sustainable Development Goals | Knowledge Platform, https://bit.ly/39JVvaW. Accessed on 23 June 2022.

environment and ethics by all stakeholders in an economy.[24]

Gandhi's ideology was highly advanced and respected the interconnectedness of the human self and ecology. Through the concept of sarvodaya, as described earlier, he successfully established an ethical and harmonious connectivity of humans with the environment. He advocated the essence of environmental ethics and the noble concept of service for common welfare based on the moral understanding of non-possession. The essence of Gandhian philosophy gradually started appearing globally in various environmental initiatives undertaken by civil society and multilateral organizations.

Till the 1960s, no major initiatives were taken considering the environment or its conservation. The oil crises of the 1970s, followed by the global financial crises of the 1980s, led to the emergence of ecological movements across the globe. Gradually, ecological movements became political movements. In 1972, the Club of Rome published a report titled *The Limits to Growth*. The Brandt Commission published *North-South: A Programme for Survival* in 1980, emphasizing on self-fulfilment and creative partnership in the use of a nation's productive forces and its full human potential. In 1983, the World Commission on Environment and Development was established. In 1992, the Earth Summit at Rio de Janeiro produced several agreements including the Rio Declaration on Environment and Development.[25] This

---

[24]Kell, George, 'The Remarkable Rise of ESG', *Forbes*, 11 July 2018, https://bit.ly/3OisQZl. Accessed on 23 June 2022.

[25]Daptardar, Vaidehi, Dr, 'Gandhian relevance to environmental sustainability', Bombay Sarvodaya Mandal & Gandhi Research Foundation, https://bit.ly/3OvaNyO. Accessed on 23 June 2022.

was followed by the Kyoto Protocol being adopted in 1997 by the United Nations Framework Convention on Climate Change.

Later, several movements and initiatives were undertaken to sensitize countries and societies about the emerging global challenge of climate change. Various non-state actors and civil society organizations collaborated vertically and horizontally at regional, national and international levels. In 2006, the *Living Planet Report* categorically stated that the lifestyle followed by western societies disturbed the subtle balance of the planet earth.[26] Later, in 2007–08, *The Human Development Report* on fighting climate change emphasized on enlightenment principle that 'human progress will make the future look better than the past'.[27] TIME magazine in 2007, published 'The Global Warming Survival Guide: 51 Things We Can Do to Save The Environment' and the fifty-first point mentioned consuming less for a simplified life.[28] We can learn to live simply so that others can simply live. The concept of 'Earth community' was adopted by Prof. Herbert Girardet in his book, *Surviving the Century: Facing the Climate Chaos.*[29]

In India, several environmental movements that took place were strictly aligned with the Gandhian belief system related to ecology and the environment. The

---

[26]Ibid

[27]Ibid.

[28]'51 Things We Can Do to Save the Environment', TIME, https://bit.ly/3Q3gViG. Accessed on 2 August 2022.

[29]Herbret, Girardet (ed.), *Surviving the Century: Facing Climate Chaos and Other Global Challenges,* Routledge, 2008.

Chipko Movement in India in the 1970s, also known as Chipko Andolan, was a non-violent social and ecological movement by rural villagers. In that movement, the voice of women became evident for saving trees and forests. Later, Narmada Bachao Andolan began in 1985—it was a social movement by native tribals, farmers, environmentalists and human rights activists. This movement was initiated against a large number of dam projects across the Narmada River. The campaign was completely non-violent, followed by hunger strikes, rallies and public gatherings. The protesters raised questions related to ownership of Chilika Lake, destruction of livelihood and commercial use of resources to close down the Coca-Cola factory in Odisha.[30]

Gandhi opposed to the western idea that considered humans as entities conquering the earth. He strongly supported Indian traditions, wherein the earth was considered as a mother. Gandhi contended that 'man has no power to create life, therefore, he has no right to destroy life'. Humans have higher intellect, so that they can be empathetic, compassionate and responsible for lower beings.[31] Gandhi demonstrated several methods of conservation of resources in day-to-day life in ashram. He used the river water sparingly even though it was in abundance, stating the rationale of non-possession or *aparigraha*. In another instance, he promoted

---

[30]Moolakkattu, John S., 'Gandhi at 150: Green Movements Have Gandhian Streak', *Down to Earth*, 1 October 2019, https://bit.ly/3HL9Vns. Accessed on 23 June 2022.

[31]Rajagopalan, M.R., 'The Environmental Crisis and Relevance of Gandhiji', Gandhi Seva Ashram, https://bit.ly/3N97uwg. Accessed on 23 June 2022.

the use of scrap papers for writing brief notes and inside-out envelopes for letters.[32] Such remarkable preaching and messages for recycling waste and conservation of resources can be related to our everyday lives.

The notion of continuity of life was maintained by Gandhian philosophy of non-violence and truth. This phenomenon of the cycle of life is similar to the fundamental theory of 'cradle to cradle' developed by Prof. Michael Braungart and William McDonough in 2001.[33] The continuity of life functions by coordinated and dedicated efforts manifested out of absolute love and empathy towards each other and nature.

Gandhi contended, 'I do believe that all God's creatures have the right to live as much as we have.'[34] He also said, 'It takes the human being beyond his species. The cow to me means the entire sub-human world. Man, through the cow, is enjoined to realise his identity with all that lives.'[35] He argued, 'I believe in Advaita (non-duaity), I believe in the essential unity of man and for that matter of all that lives. Therefore I believe that if one man gains spiritually, the whole world gains with him and if one man fails, the whole world fails to that extent.'[36]

---

[32]Sheth, Pravin, 'The Eco-Gandhi and Ecological Movements', Gandhi Sevagram Ashram, https://bit.ly/3HOSAdu. Accessed on 24 June 2022.

[33]McDonough, William and Michael Braungart, *Cradle to Cradle: Remaking the Way We Make Things*, North Point Press, 2002.

[34]Gandhi, Mohandas K., *Harijan Vol. 4: 1936-1937*, Navajivan Publishing House, 2013.

[35]*Young India*, 6 October 1921.

[36]Weber, Thomas, 'Gandhi and Deep Ecology', *Journal of Peace Research,* May 1996, Vol. 30, No. 3. https://bit.ly/3NikIH7. Accessed on 24 June 2022.

However, human civilization missed out on this underlying connectivity between man and nature as a part of the cycle of life and spirituality. The impact of humanity on the environment and the resulting inequalities are evident in climate change. This biggest global challenge finds a direct linkage to the use of conventional energy sources and unchecked economic growth.

Climate change, energy, environment and ecology are all intertwined and interconnected. Ignoring energy in the gambit of the climate change debate would be a blunder; not bringing in the arguments of the Gandhian perspective related to energy will not complete the Gandhian revolution or paradigm. Countries across the globe are struggling to achieve carbon-neutral economies in the present scenario, in which they are confronted by the global challenge of climate change.

The centralized energy system has been exploitative and destructive to the environment, leading to concentration and preponderance of power, vested interests, war and unrest. The indispensable political economy associated with conventional energy has resulted in inequality, injustice and climate change. The world has realized the immense need to undergo a paradigm shift in the energy regime, also referred to as the energy transition, is inevitable. United Nations Sustainable Development Goals (SDGs), adopted in 2015, have been dedicated to incorporating challenges related to energy.[37] Improved access to energy, renewable

[37]'Do You Know All 17 SDGs?', United Nations | Department of Economic and Social Affairs, https://bit.ly/3tZvY4m. Accessed on 24 June 2022.

energy and energy efficiency have been discussed in the SDGs.

Gandhi believed socio-economic systems should follow that decentralized way of functioning. A decentralized energy system will lead to more flexibility in generation and meeting the local demand patterns for electricity and heat. This also implies greater awareness of energy issues through community-based energy systems, driving change in social attitudes and more efficient use of energy resources. Locally confined social set-ups and communities, which are self-sufficient and based on local resources, lead to lesser consumption.

An ethically enlightened and morally evolved socio-economic decentralized Gandhian setting will lead to the ethical use of energy resources. Moreover, the energy demand in such communities will be need-based and not dependent on unlimited wants or desires. Limited consumption, consensus-based, self-sufficient and energy-independent communities reflect a Gandhian ethical revolution.

The Gandhian ethical and moral revolution uplifts the individual self and elevates the human value system. The inner self of an individual gets transformed to seek the absolute truth and becomes enlightened with empathy and love for humankind. Non-violence, peace and tolerance are the fundamentals of the ethically evolved self. Therefore, the desired benefits of such a revolution are not confined to only one individual but are manifested in humankind as a whole. Such a Gandhian moral revolution transforms the inner self and formulates connectivity amidst humans. It is this transformation that revolutionizes socio-economic and political relations, which referred to as Gandhian economic revolution and Gandhian political revolution, respectively, as described in the chapters. Finally, the Gandhian moral revolution strives to achieve unity and oneness in ecological harmony, and that is referred to as the Gandhian ecological revolution.

ONE

Gandhian Moral Revolution

It was with Mahatma Gandhi that something new made its appearance in modern moral philosophy. The Gandhian moral revolution was indeed revolutionary, since it transformed the whole relation between the definition of civilization and the architecture of ethics. Civilization, Gandhi wrote in 1909 in his seminal work, *Hind Swaraj*, 'is that mode of conduct which points out to man the path of duty. Performance of duty and observance of morality are convertible terms. To observe morality is to attain mastery over our mind and our passions. So doing, we know ourselves'.[1] As such, the core idea that emerged from the first experience of satyagraha, which was in South Africa, was that of self-mastery. Gandhi was, above all, concerned with the Socrates's use of the Delphic maxim 'know thyself' as a necessary moral element of what he underlined as swaraj or self-rule.

An outspoken philosopher and an ethical parrhesiast, Socrates exhorted Athenian citizens to be concerned not for wealth and power, but for the welfare of their souls. As a

[1]Gandhi, M.K., *'Hind Swaraj' and Other Writings*, Anthony J. Parel (ed.), Cambridge University Press, Cambridge, 1997, p. 67.

matter of fact, it was Socrates's ethics of self-examination that prevented him from acting wrongly. His abstention from untruth and injustice was a philosophical act, which permitted him to follow his daimon, his inner voice, in direct opposition to the prejudices of the masses.

> [I]nner experience was extraordinary. [He] heard a voice inaudible to anyone else. In some situations, the voice ordered him to halt what he was doing and to change his course of conduct. According to Plato, our primary source for almost everything we think we know about the first philosopher, Socrates considered the voice to be uniquely his own, as if it were directed to him alone from a supernatural sort of tutelary spirit. A source of wonder and disquiet, the voice set Socrates apart. From the time he was a child, he felt isolated and different—an individual in a collective that prized its sense of community, vividly expressed in its web of customary rituals and traditional religious beliefs, and crowned by a set of political institutions that embodied the novel ideal of democracy, a new form of collective self-rule.[2]

Socrates's appeal to his inner voice strengthened him morally and philosophically; his moral integrity made him a lover of wisdom par excellence. In other words, Socrates's commitment to live philosophically in truth was the direct outcome of his understanding of the ethical nature of his actions. Socrates knew that a life worth living is the one

---

[2]Miller, James, *Examined Lives: From Socrates to Nietzsche*, Farrar, Straus, and Giroux, New York, 2011, p. 20.

that is guided by the pursuit of wisdom and the ethical content of philosophical questioning. Over the centuries, this Socratic moment of questioning and self-examination has been endorsed by all those who have maintained that unjust laws are contrary to the higher law of moral conscience. Historically speaking, no person as Gandhi has been so close to the Socratic moral ideas of self-examination and self-realization.

The concept of self-rule, as presented in Gandhi's thoughts, offers the possibility to express the core aims of integral Socratic ethics. Like Socrates, Gandhi strived to live a life of wisdom that suggested self-examination and promoted moral values. However, the path Gandhi tried to trace as an Indian philosopher and politician not only passed through a non-violent struggle but also through a new paradigm of human progress. As such, Gandhi considered the civilizing process, more than anything else, a test of moral strength. He located the basic malaise of modern civilization in its immoral thirst for wealth and material pleasure. According to Gandhi:

> A civilization that is based on greed, in which mammon has replaced God, which measures progress in terms of profits, which puts corporate health and the stock market above human health and well-being can hardly be called a civilization. A civilization that has destroyed the environment and threatens the very existence of the planet can surely not be considered progressive.[3]

---

[3]Kaul, J.M., 'Hind Swaraj: Hundred Years After How Relevant is it Today?' *Reflections on Hind Swaraj*, Siby K. Joseph and Bharat Mahodaya (eds.), Institute of Gandhian Studies, Wardha, 2011, pp. 166–7.

In other words, 'The philosophy implicit in modern/western civilization is the hedonistic philosophy of maximizing pleasure and minimizing pain.'[4]

Gandhi's questioning of utilitarian and instrumentalist rationality, as practised by European modernity, was followed with the idea of non-violence as the only morally and politically acceptable alternative to it. That is to say, Gandhi's critique of modern civilization in *Hind Swaraj* is one of the greatest Socratic gestures of moral dissent in the history of modern thought. Accordingly, what Gandhi suggested was a moral revolution: Socratic self-examination accompanied by self-transformation of society. In that sense, we can find in the Gandhian moral philosophy a close connection between political self-rule and ethical self-transformation of the individual. In this, Gandhi was a total follower of Socrates, since he admired Socrates's moral courage and his practice of soul force. Maybe that is why, Gandhi considered Socrates as a satyagrahi and a soldier of truth. In South Africa, Gandhi published an article on Socrates in the columns of the *Indian Opinion*, titled 'Story of a Soldier of Truth'. In this article, Gandhi described Socrates as 'heroic' and wrote: 'Today, the world cherishes Socrates's memory. His teaching has benefited millions. His accusers and his judges stand condemned by the world. Socrates has gained immortality and Greece stands in high esteem because of him and others like him.'[5] Like Socrates,

---

[4]Ibid.

[5]*The Collected Works of Mahatma Gandhi, Vol. VIII, January–August 1908*, The Publications Division, Ministry of Information and Broadcasting, Government of India, 1962, p. 173.

Gandhi was a philosopher of civic dissent, who found the source of his action in his moral conscience. This is how we can understand Gandhi's reference to his 'inner voice' as an experience of living in truth. For Gandhi, the 'still small voice', as he called it, was always the final arbiter in his diverse conflicts in life. He also called it the voice of conscience or the voice of God. Speaking of his experience with this inner voice, in 1933, he wrote in *Harijan*:

> For me the voice of God, of Conscience, of Truth, or the Inner Voice or 'the still small voice' mean one and the same thing. I saw no form. Have never tried, for I have always believed God to be without form. But what I did hear was like a Voice from afar and yet quite near. It was as unmistakable as some human voice definitely speaking to me, and irresistible. I was not dreaming at the time I heard the Voice. The hearing of the Voice was preceded by a terrific struggle within me. Suddenly the voice came upon me. I listened, made certain it was the Voice, and the struggle ceased.[6]

Gandhi's appeal to his 'inner voice' was in many ways similar to Socrates's dialogue with his daimon. For both Socrates and Gandhi, the aim of the appeal was to discover a path to truth, while purifying one's heart and preparing oneself against the violence of the political realm. Speaking of morality as an ideal, Gandhi affirmed, 'So far as I know my own conscience I have myself striven through thought, word

[6] *Harijan*, 8 July 1933, p. 4.

and deed to reach the ideal.'[7] As such Gandhi positioned himself closer to Socrates and his philosophy as a source of moral virtue. He argued, 'We pray to God, and want our readers also to pray, that they, and we too, may have the moral strength which enabled Socrates to follow virtue to the end and to embrace death as if it were his beloved. We advise everyone to turn his mind again and again to Socrates' words and conduct.'[8]

For Gandhi, Socrates's moral courage and quest for excellence affirmed the importance of self-realization and non-violent conscience as foundations of his political philosophy. Thus, it is all the more necessary to point out that Gandhi's critical attitude toward modern civilization in *Hind Swaraj* is the direct result of his moral proximity with Socrates's practical philosophy.

Going back to *Hind Swaraj*, we can say that Gandhi considered modern western civilization as immoral and irreligious, having no quest for self-sacrifice and love for the others. He wrote:

> This civilization takes note neither of morality nor of religion. Its votaries calmly state that their business is not to teach religion. Some even consider it to be a superstitious growth. Others put on the cloak of religion, and prate about morality. But, after twenty

---

[7]Iyer, Raghavan (ed.), *The Moral and Political Writings of Mahatma Gandhi, Vol. II*, Oxford University Press, 1986, p. 293.

[8]*The Collected Works of Mahatma Gandhi, Vol. VIII, January–August 1908*, The Publications Division, Ministry of Information and Broadcasting, Government of India, 1962, p. 229.

> years' experience, I have come to the conclusion that immorality is often taught in the name of morality. Even a child can understand that in all I have described above there can be no inducement to morality. Civilization seeks to increase bodily comforts, and it fails miserably even in doing so.[9]

Thus, Gandhi perceived a clear distinction between civilization as the path of compassionate self-realization, and civilization as a mad race for economic and technological progress. In this connection, it is important to note that Gandhi suggested diminishing the wants in order to lesser the pains caused by the modern civilization.

> That is why he advocated simple living and high thinking. High thinking comes from spiritual awakening, which boils down to love and compassion towards all. In practical terms, it means having enough to satisfy one's basic material needs, and aiming at spiritual attainment while living in this world of good and evil and working to build a civilization of peace and harmony.[10]

Mahatma Gandhi's paradigm of progress was neither defensive, nor imitative, but essentially moral and spiritual. In that sense, his idea of a modern Indian civilization differed entirely from the Turkish and Japanese plans of

---

[9]Gandhi, M.K., *'Hind Swaraj' and Other Writings*, Anthony J. Parel (ed.), Cambridge University Press, Cambridge, 1997, p. 37.

[10]Misra, R.P., *Rediscovering Gandhi: Hind Swaraj Volume 1: Gandhi's Challenge to Modern Civilization*, Concept Publishing, New Delhi, 2007, p. 42.

modernization. According to Hasan Kösebalaban, associate professor of political science at Istanbul Sehir University:

> An analysis of Turkish and Japanese cases indicates a remarkable degree of similarity in regard to their historical question of civilizational identity. Turkey and Japan faced a similar challenge from the West at the end of the nineteenth century, and similarly responded to this challenge through defensive modernization and Westernization. In turn, they experienced a similar identity shift from Asian to Western, one that transformed their perception of belonging. For both nations, this shift was an incomplete process. Turkish secularist nationalists never internalized the West completely, while Japan's quest for a recognition of equality had failed before the Second World War, leading to a new orientation of Pan-Asianism in the 1930s and 1940s. Hence Japan faces a similar problem of obscurity in their civilizational orientations, as they, like Turkey, are neither completely part of the West nor completely part of the East.[11]

First and foremost, Gandhi did not equate the modern and the western. Though Gandhi was a relentless critic of modern industrial civilization, it appears that he carefully shaped his moral and political philosophy by reading some western authors, like Leo Tolstoy, Henry David Thoreau and John Ruskin. As he asserted famously, 'I do not want

---

[11]Kosebalaban, Hasan, 'Torn Identities and Foreign Policy: The Case of Turkey and Japan', *Insight Turkey*, Vol. 10, No. 1, 2008, p. 23.

my house to be walled in on all sides and my windows to be stuffed. I want the culture of all lands to be blown about my house as freely as possible.'[12] As *Hind Swaraj* and Gandhi's autobiography show us clearly and distinctly, he did not reject the emancipative content of modernity. On the contrary, he internalized and practised the dissenting philosophies of Tolstoy, Thoreau and Ruskin.

In arguing for the ethical over the utilitarian, Gandhi argued for a process of unlearning modernity as was presented by the West. Thus, he emphasized on a strong ethical positioning of India, which would be accompanied with a new sense of self-respect, self-reliance and self-governance. Yet the ethic that Gandhi was trying to introduce and inscribe into Indian social life was an effort of living *in* and *with* truth, beyond the modern spirit of conquest and domination of colonialism. For Gandhi, truth was not a matter of cognition, but of moral experience. His autobiography, titled *My Experiments with Truth*, is surely an indication of this. Therefore, Gandhi's truth had little to do with modern science and was concerned with experimentation giving way to argument and vice versa. His truth was an experiential and spiritual one, very much in tandem with the tradition of Socrates, the Roman philosopher, Lucius Annaeus Seneca and the wise thinkers of India. Rudolf Heredia, the founder of the Social Science Centre, St Xavier's College, Mumbai, said:

> For Gandhi, *satya* was an absolute reality that we could only partially grasp. Thus the many-sidedness of truth

---

[12]Kripalani, Krishna (ed.), *All Men are Brothers*, Navajivan Publishing House, Ahmedabad, 1960, p. 199.

> that we experience is nothing but a consequence of such relative knowledge. Overcoming these limitations of our 'relative knowledge' for a more comprehensive grasp of this 'absolute truth' could never be forced by violence. Only ahimsa, non-violence, could make the quest for such truth viable. Gandhi operationalised this quest in his strategy of satyagraha, or truth-force. Moreover, he makes no ethical separation between means and an end. Both must be morally good.[13]

The Gandhian moral revolution, therefore, took shape at several levels. The whole Gandhian approach to history, as a manifestation of moral progress of humanity, was a new way of understanding the constituting elements of a 'common humanity'. Therefore, Gandhi's emphasis on solidarity among human beings shows quite well that he was not in search for individual liberation. In fact, he wrote:

> I do not believe...that an individual may gain spiritually and those who surround him suffer. I believe in Advaita, I believe in the essential unity of man and, for that matter, of all that life's. Therefore, I believe that if one man gains spiritually, the whole world gains with him and, if one man falls, the whole world falls to that extent.[14]

---

[13]Heredia, Rudolf C., 'Interpreting Gandhi's Hind Swaraj', *Economic and Political Weekly*, June 12–18, 1999, Vol. 34, No. 24, p. 1499.

[14]Weber, Thomas, 'Gandhi's Moral Economics: The Sins of Wealth without Work and Commerce without Morality', *The Cambridge Companion to Gandhi*, Judith Brown and Anthony Parel (eds.), Cambridge University Press, Cambridge, 2011, p. 150.

Gandhi's stress on unity of humankind helps us understand not only his moral effort to salvage the Indian self from the colonial rule but also redefine a new relationship between the individual and the society, shaped by internal moral power rather than rational violence. Gandhi's philosophy was a result of a search for realistic harmony between means and ends on the basis of such moral empowerment. Gandhi's genuine concern for the common good and his moral vision of social reality was ultimately the reminder of his examination of the frailty of the human social condition. That is why Gandhi was very firm in his rejection of the rigid dichotomy between ends and means.

Gandhi developed his view of the relationship between the means and ends in the form of the following statement: 'They say "means are after all means". I would say "means are after all everything". As the means so the end.'[15] In other words, the separation of the social, as the art of interacting, and the ethical, as the ability to live in truth with the other, would have been unacceptable to Gandhi. Responding to fellow Indians, who believed in the use of violence against the British, Gandhi responded:

> Your belief that there is no connection between the means and the end is a great mistake. Through that mistake, even men who have been considered religious have committed grievous crimes. Your reasoning is the same as saying that we can get a rose through planting a noxious weed. If I want to cross the ocean, I can do

[15]Kripalani, Krishna (ed.), *All Men are Brothers*, Navajivan Publishing House, Ahmedabad, 1960, p. 134.

> so only by means of a vessel; if I were to use a cart for that purpose, both the cart and I would soon find the bottom. 'As is the God, so is the votary' is a maxim worth considering. Its meaning has been distorted and men have gone astray. The means may be likened to a seed, the end to a tree; and there is just the same inviolable connection between the means and the end as there is between the seed and the tree.[16]

As we can see, Gandhi paid great attention to the relation between means and ends, as he believed that empathetic interconnectedness was essentially the appreciation of the moral role of an individual in society. So, a truly inclusive and non-violent society should be understood in terms of means and not the end because only individual actors have the power to change history. In that sense, Gandhi's view of non-violent citizenship was first and foremost ethical because it grew from the individual's moral conscience and not from the political or judicial rules of the system.

However, it would be wrong to consider Gandhi's critique of violence as a passive response to all forms of realism. Gandhi described himself as a 'practical idealist', but we can also represent him as an 'ethical realist'. Karuna Mantena, who specializes in political theory, argues correctly:

> In Gandhi, we can see how tethering political potentiality to the given constraints of political life does not entail an a priori restriction on imaginative possibilities; it only insists on scrupulous attention

[16]Ibid. 135.

> to the means of working out from and through these constraints toward envisioned ends. In this form of realism, the ends and goals of political life may even be high-minded, demanding, and radical (as surely many of Gandhi's were), but the means for the effectuation of norms cannot be left unspecified and, hence, unreal. In this manner, with Gandhi, political realism can perhaps be rescued from its association with amoral instrumentalism and status quo politics and instead be viewed as offering an alternative way of thinking pointedly and precisely about the conditions for effective and principled political action.[17]

As a matter of fact, one of the dimensions of Gandhian realism was 'the idea of perishing for a cause, for other men, for a village even'.[18] In other words, Gandhi 'had always held that satyagraha implied the willingness to accept not only suffering but also death for the sake of a principle'.[19] Gandhi's dedication to truth, even in the face of death, was an example of his moral courage. Once again, we find here a Gandhian idea, which constituted a challenge to all ethical and political currents in modern civilization and undermined the question of self-sacrifice and self-suffering.

Truly, for Gandhi, self-sacrifice and self-suffering were very often considered public acts in order to publicize his

---

[17]Mantena, Karuna, 'Another Realism: The Politics of Gandhian Nonviolence', *American Political Science Review*, May 2012, Vol. 106, No. 2, p. 468.

[18]Woodcock, George, *Gandhi*, Fontana, London, 1972, p. 96.

[19]Ibid.

moral philosophy against what he considered morally wrong and evil. As such, he saw fasting as a strong means against violence. Bidyut Chakrabarty, vice chancellor at Visva-Bharati in West Bengal, said:

> In Gandhian *satyagraha*, fasting, which was purificatory as well, was defined 'as a great weapon in the armoury of satyagraha.' Gandhi also undertook fasts to put pressure on his opponents when persuasion failed to yield results. This was a device to inflict pain on himself, a process that Gandhi believed would persuade his opponents to appreciate the goals for which the fast was undertaken.[20]

Gandhi fasted many times to repent for the violence perpetrated by the Indian masses during the Indian struggle for independence. His five-day fast in February 1922 against the police violence in the Chauri Chaura incident and his fast unto death in January 1948 for communal harmony are among the most famous ethical actions of his life. Clearly, for Gandhi, the act of fasting was a dissenting act against ideas and institutions, which were unjust in his eyes. However, it also represented a mode of critical questioning of his own judgement and that of the others. Interestingly, Gandhi knew that *The Story of My Experiments with Truth* was the work of a lonely moral consciousness. Loneliness was one of the fundamental existential features of Gandhian moral courage.

---

[20]Chakrabarty, Bidyut, *Social and Political Thought of Mahatma Gandhi*, Routledge, 2006, p. 68.

For Gandhi, a true satyagrahi was always expected to take a position independent of those in power and sometimes in direct opposition to the opinions of the masses. As a matter of fact, Gandhi's spiritual courage was always backed up by the mental and physical capabilities of an autonomous individual who was often lonely because of his attentiveness to the moral disquiet within him. There is an anecdote, presented by Ravindra Varma, about Gandhi's confrontation with the fury of a mob after the partition of India:

> For many years since Gandhi came back to India from South Africa it was impossible for him to travel anywhere in India or address meetings without being mobbed by devotees who were eager to catch a glimpse, to reach his hands to deposit jewellery or money in donations, or to touch his feet. But after Partition, there were many occasions on which Gandhi had to face the fury of those who had been displaced or looted, or dishonoured. On his way to Kashmir, Gandhi passed through Amritsar. As his train drew in on the platform, the air was rent with cries of 'Gandhi go back.' A hundred or more young men with black flags came and stood opposite the compartment in which Gandhi was travelling. Amidst cries of 'Gandhi go back,' they started pounding the panels and the body of the compartment. They peeped in, glowed at Gandhi, shouted themselves hoarse, and threw sticks (on which black flags had been mounted) into the compartment. In the midst of the deafening din, and the faces glowing with fury, stood Gandhi. He had plugged his ears with his fingers, and was looking at

> the irate young men with calm eyes that reflected his compassion and agony.[21]

Gandhi was well aware of the fact that non-violence is a difficult and daunting task. But, he also knew that it is a never-ending quest for excellence and exemplarity. He saw non-violence as the narrow distance that humankind had created between itself and barbarism. He knew well that if human beings wanted to live in a world that practised non-violence, they would have to believe in moral life as the nobility of human spirit.[22] We can find here, once again, Gandhi's explicit reference to the idea of self-sacrifice and self-suffering as forms of moral courage. However, one can also find a direct hint to the concept of maturity. In other words, according to Gandhi, the main process by which an individual is inwardly cultivated is that of coming to maturity in ever-greater depth. As such, Gandhi's moral exemplarity and the question of ethical maturity that concerned him all his life could be analysed as an ethical mode of being, which enabled the Indian society to become conscious of its plurality and discover the criteria of interconnectedness. Accordingly, Gandhian moral revolution propelled the Indian society, in particular, and humanity in general to a new and deep understanding of the concept of interdependence. For Gandhi, empathy was an agency and a transformative

---

[21]Varma, Ravindra, *Gandhi in Anecdotes*, Navajivan Publishing House, Ahmedabad, 2001, pp. 176–7.

[22]*The Collected Works of Mahatma Gandhi, Vol. XVIII, July–November 1920,* The Publications Division, Ministry of Information and Broadcasting, Government of India, 1965, pp. 50–1.

force—an experience of moral conscience underpinning the harmony between the individual and the universe.

Gandhi was thinking in terms of long-term non-violent social relations among individuals and perpetual peace among nations. So, he wanted to put his hands on the wheel of history, through his empathetic ethics, in order to move from private desires to public responsibilities, and from national and religious prejudices to a cosmic fellowship. Consequently, the Gandhian appeal to the ethics of empathy was not only a way to know oneself in ever-greater depth but was also a cultivation of one's capacity for global responsibility. Ultimately, what was important for Gandhi was to give a paramount place to morality in all our affairs, be those national or international. He wrote in *Harjan* on 8 June 1940: 'Morality which depends upon the helplessness of a man or woman has not much to recommend it. Morality is rooted in the purity of our hearts.'[23]

Gandhi was thinking in terms of a common humanity, which could transcend the rule of modern violence through its moral nature. Surprisingly, he was well aware of the originality of this moral imperative during his campaigns on civil disobedience and non-violent resistance in South Africa. On 5 January 1907, he wrote in the columns of the *Indian Opinion*:

> It is the moral nature of man by which he rises to good and noble thoughts. The different sciences show

---

[23] *The Collected Works of Mahatma Gandhi, Vol. LXXII, April 16–September 11, 1940*, The Publications Division, Ministry of Information and Broadcasting, Government of India, 1978, p. 137.

> us the world as it is. Ethics tells us what it ought to be. It enables man to know how he should act. Man has two windows to his mind: through one he can see his own self as it is; through the other, he can see what it ought to be. It is our task to analyse and explore the body, the brain and the mind of man separately; but if we stop here, we derive no benefit despite our scientific knowledge. It is necessary to know about the evil effects of injustice, wickedness, vanity and the like, and the disaster they spell where the three are found together. And mere knowledge is not enough, it should be followed by appropriate action. An ethical idea is like an architect's plan. The plan shows how the building should be constructed; but it becomes useless if the building is not raised accordingly. Similarly, an ethical idea is useless so long as it is not followed by suitable action... In the path of morality there is no such thing as reward for moral behaviour. If a man does some good deed, he does not do it to win applause, he does it because he must. For him doing good is but a higher kind of food, if one may compare food and goodness.[24]

It is crucial for our understanding of Gandhian moral revolution to realize the significance of a moral act as a basic principle in living together and self-transformation of the individual and society. Moreover, Gandhi, unlike many moral theorists of his time, sought to provide an

---

[24]*The Collected Works of Mahatma Gandhi, Vol. VI, 1906–1907*, The Publications Division, Ministry of Information and Broadcasting, Government of India, 1961, p. 275.

alternative vision to the utilitarian and materialistic scopes of modernity. He argued:

> A moral act must be our own act; it must spring from our own will. If we act mechanically, there is no moral content in our act. Such action would be moral, if we think it proper to act like a machine and do so. For in doing so, we use our discrimination. We should bear in mind the distinction between acting mechanically and acting intentionally. It may be a moral of a king to pardon a culprit. But the messenger bearing the order of pardon plays only a mechanical part in the king's moral act... Just as a moral action should be free from fear or compulsion so should there be no self-interest behind it. This is not to say that actions prompted by self-interest are all worthless, but only that to call them moral would detract from the [dignity of the] moral idea.[25]

As Gandhi's moral thought matured, he placed increasing emphasis on swaraj as moral uplift. Gandhi argued, until the end of his life, that moral autonomy is not only about the acquisition of 'inward freedom' but also the attainment of a level of moral maturity, which could make individuals and nations aware of their interdependence and indebtedness to each other. No argument was to become more central than this to Gandhian moral revolution. Dennis Dalton's *Mahatma Gandhi: Nonviolent Power in Action* reads: '"I value individual freedom," Gandhi remarked, "but you must not forget that man is essentially a social being," and

[25]Ibid. 284–5.

"unrestricted individualism" must be curtailed by social conscience "to strike the mean between individual freedom and social restraint".'[26]

No doubt, for Gandhi, the only way to form the political, attain and sustain a democracy was through a revolution of values. From Gandhi's perspective, democracy was a political imagination that arose from the moral interdependence of humanity. Therefore, Gandhi advocated for an awareness of the essential moral imperative that called for a move from egocentricity and utilitarian greed towards a 'shared humanity'. As such, Gandhi reminded his fellow Indians and others that a common humanity cannot exist if it is not aware of its shortcomings. Consequently, the Gandhian lesson of empathetic ethics is still relevant for today's world since humanity needs to strive to remove its ethical imperfections in order to be able to live with the global challenges it faces. Therefore, in an age of increasing 'globalization of selfishness', there is an urgent need to understand and practise the moral revolution suggested by Gandhi, and try to re-evaluate the concept of politics in the shadow of the Gandhian paradigm.

Being a genuine democrat, Gandhi stood, all his life, for a non-violent and empathetic mode of conduct, as the definite way towards self-rule and individual freedom. He knew well that 'the first step to *Swaraj* lies in the individual'.[27] Hence, he tried to show that 'political self-government that is self-government for large number of men

---

[26]Dalton, Dennis, *Mahatma Gandhi: Nonviolent Power in Action*, Columbia University Press, New York, 1993, p. 198.

[27]*Speeches and Writings of M.K. Gandhi*, G.A. Natesan & Co., Madras, 1922, p. 381.

and women, is no better than individual self-government, and, therefore, it is to be attained by precisely the same means that are required for individual self-government or self-rule'.[28] This implied a moral and political connection between the personal and the public that Gandhi discussed extensively in his philosophy of swaraj. In other words, along with his moral revolution, the most important theoretical change generated by Gandhi's paradigm was his political revolution. His vision for Indian self-rule was more than that of a democratic India. He had underlined the essence of his political revolution in *Hind Swaraj*, and his search for swaraj continued after his return to India in 1915. This pursuit of moral self-realization and political self-governance transformed the whole conception of power in modern political theory.

[28]Desai, Mahadev H., *With Gandhiji in Ceylon: A Journal of the Tour with Authorised Version of all Important Speeches*, S. Ganesan, Madras, 1928, p. 93.

TWO

Gandhian Political Revolution

The development of Gandhi's thoughts regarding the concept of swaraj, after his arrival in India in January 1915, should be considered as one of the main pillars of Gandhian political revolution.

As striking as it might appear, his contribution to modern political theory rested on his understanding and practice of truthfulness and self-rule in public life. In that sense, his vision of politics was very similar to that in ancient Greek and quite different from the liberal or socialist views of his contemporaries.

As in the case of his moral ideas, Gandhi's political ideas can be already found in *Hind Swaraj*. One of his principle ideas in the book was that India, being a political entity, had the right to self-government. This was because Gandhi, like Aristotle, considered politics as the highest form of *vita activa* (active life). For him, Indians could have self-rule as individuals and self-governance as a nation only if they became truthful and underwent a suitable degree of self-transformation. Anthony Parel, author and historian, said:

> Gandhi draws a subtle distinction between Swaraj as self-rule and Swaraj as self-government or home rule. Swaraj as self-rule is the rule of the self by the self.

> More precisely, it is the rule of the mind over itself and the passions—the passions of greed and aggression, in particular... Swaraj as self-government or home rule is the rule of the nation (*praja*) by the nation. It is the founding and maintaining of the good state (*surajya*). The good state or good self-government is possible only if Indians acquire the capacity for self-rule, but self-rule itself can flourish only within an appropriate political community.[29]

Gandhi's insistence on the concept of 'community' as the basis of democratic life is the key to understanding his discourse on swaraj. In the Gandhian scheme, the idea of 'community' must focus on the principles of truthfulness and love. The way to swaraj is largely dependent on an empathetic community that walks the path of truthfulness and love in day-to-day life. That is why Gandhi considered *Hind Swaraj* 'a book which can be put into the hands of a child [Because] it teaches the gospel of love in place of that of hate. It replaces violence with self-sacrifice. It pits soul-force against brute-force...'[30] As such, Gandhi did not follow the general conception that India would attain home rule by overthrowing the British Raj. Actually, Gandhi's greatest problem was not the British, but the Indians. Gandhi, therefore, argued: 'You want the tiger's nature, but not the tiger; that is to say, you would make India English, and

---

[29]Gandhi, M.K., '*Hind Swaraj' and Other Writings*, Anthony J. Parel (ed.), Cambridge University Press, Cambridge, 1997, pp. lii-liii.

[30]Fischer, Louis (ed.), *The Essential Gandhi: An Anthology of His Writings on His Life, Work, and Ideas*, Vintage Books, New York, 1983, p. 104.

when it becomes English, it will be called not Hindustan but Englistan. This is not the Swaraj that I want.'[31] We can see here not only a Gandhian criticism of the British colonial rule, but a conscientious and rigorous analysis of the modern liberal doctrine. As such, Gandhi's conception of swaraj was neither a liberal approach to politics nor a simple third-worldist decolonizing effort.

> Gandhi's concept of *Swaraj* is not merely a form of governance. It is an all comprehensive concept encompassing all spheres of life. At the individual level it means self-refinement or purification for higher goals of life. Politically, *Swaraj* is the sovereignty of the people based on pure moral authority. Economically, Swaraj means self-reliant and self-sufficient economy. And in the ultimate sense, it is self-rule or self-restraint aimed at *moksha* or salvation. In the Gandhian conception *Swaraj* is freedom from all forms of control.[32]

We need to understand that Gandhi was not a typical practitioner of party politics; he was in favour of a decentralized and anti-bureaucratic form of governance. In other words, Gandhi's critique of the dark side of political modernity, defined by the two concepts of conquest and domination, was accompanied by an effort to change the heart, and mind, of Indians. For him, self-rule was a highly moral

---

[31]Gandhi, M.K., '*Hind Swaraj' and Other Writings*, Anthony J. Parel (ed.), Cambridge University Press, Cambridge, 1997, p. 28

[32]Joseph, Siby K., 'Swaraj and Governance', *Reflections on Hind Swaraj*, Siby K. Joseph and Bharat Mahodaya (eds.), Institute of Gandhian Studies, Wardha, 2011, p. 197.

practice. Therefore, Gandhi, unlike many thinkers of modern politics, saw an element of truthfulness and righteousness in the shaping process of swaraj. As he underlined:

> Swaraj and Ramrajya are one and the same thing... We call a State Ramrajya when both the ruler and his subjects are straight forward, when both are pure in heart, when both are inclined towards self-sacrifice, when both exercise restraint and self-control while enjoying worldly pleasures, and, when the relationship between the two is as good as that between father and son. It is because we have forgotten this that we talk of democracy or the government of the people. Although this is the age of democracy, I do not know what the word connotes; however, I would say that democracy exists where the people's voice is heard, where love of the people holds a place of prime importance. In my Ramrajya, however, public opinion cannot be measured by counting of heads or raising of hands. I would not regard this as a measure of public opinion... The rishis and munis after doing penance came to the conclusion that public opinion is the opinion of people who practise penance and who have the good of the people at heart.[33]

Since Gandhi believed in a non-violent emancipation of India, his ideal of swaraj was based on self-sufficient and self-reliant village republics. As he wrote in *Harijan* in 1942:

---

[33] *Collected Works of Mahatma Gandhi, Vol. XXXV, September 1927–January 1928*, The Publications Division, Ministry of Information and Broadcasting, Government of India, 1969, pp. 489–90.

> My idea of Village *Swaraj* is that it is a complete republic, independent of its neighbours for its own vital wants, and yet interdependent for many others in which dependence is a necessity. Thus every village's first concern will be to grow its own food crops and cotton for its cloth... There will be no castes such as we have today with their graded untouchability. Non-violence with its technique of Satyagraha and non-co-operation will be the sanction of the village community... The government of the village will be conducted by the Panchayat of five persons, annually elected by the adult villagers, male and female, possessing minimum prescribed qualifications. These will have all the authority and jurisdiction required. Since there will be no system of punishments in the accepted sense, this Panchayat will be the legislature, judiciary and executive combined to operate for its year of office... Here there is perfect democracy based upon individual freedom. The individual is the architect of his own government. The law of non-violence rules him and his government. He and his village are able to defy the might of a world.[34]

Gandhi envisaged a limited state reduced to minimum of bureaucracy. At the same time, he believed that politics should focus on the life of the most disadvantaged and not only be the mirror of the Indian nomenclature. As he said:

---

[34]Gandhi, M.K., *Village Swaraj*, H.M. Vyas (ed.), Navajivan Publishing House, Ahmedabad, 1963, pp. 31–2.

> Whenever you are in doubt, or when the self becomes too much with you, apply the following test. Recall the face of the poorest and the weakest man whom you may have seen, and ask yourself if the step you contemplate is going to be of any use to him. Will he gain anything by it? Will it restore him to a control over his own life and destiny? In other words, will it lead to swaraj for the hungry and spiritually starving millions.[35]

Consequently, Gandhi considered politics as an art of organizing society by empowering the powerless. In that, politics helped the individual realize themself by aspiring for truth in life. Accordingly, Gandhi's model of politics was not in service of any particular ideology, religion or political party. Gandhi envisioned politics as a tool for self-organizing the public space for individuals. From the Gandhian point of view, political self-rule went hand in hand with individual self-realization and self-regulation. However, Gandhi saw self-realization of the individual not simply as a right but also as a duty. He observed:

> In Swaraj based on Ahimsa, people need not know their rights, but it is necessary for them to know their duties. There is no duty but creates a corresponding right, and those only are true rights which flow from a due performance of one's duties. Hence rights of true citizenship accrue only to those who serve the State to which they belong. And they alone can do justice

[35]Parel, Anthony J. (ed.), *Gandhi, Freedom and Self-Rule*, Lexington Books, 2000, p. 15.

> to the rights that accrue to them. Everyone possesses the right to tell lies or resort to goondasim. But the exercise of such a right is harmful both to the exerciser and society. But to him who observes Truth and Non-violence comes prestige, and prestige brings rights. And people who obtain rights as a result of performance of duty, exercise them only for the service of society, never for themselves. Swaraj of a people means the sum total of the Swaraj (self-rule) of individuals. And such Swaraj comes only from performance by individuals of their duty as citizens. In it, no one thinks of his rights. They come, when they are needed, for better performance of duty.[36]

Thus, for Gandhi, politics was a state of mind and a mode of being where one had the capacity to actualize their duty in regard to others. Therefore, he considered rights as an outcome of duties and not vice versa. In contrast to the liberal theory of rights, he insisted on prioritizing duties over rights. In his view, duties were more important in moral and political actions because they were based on the process of seeking truth. This appeal to the notion of duty entered the scene very early in his political action. He put accent on the concepts of duty and rights in Chapter XVI of *Hind Swaraj*. Gandhi affirmed:

> Real rights are a result of performance of duty; these rights they have not obtained. We, therefore, have

[36]Gandhi, Mahatma, *Selected Political Writings*, Dennis Dalton (ed.), Hackett Publishing, Indiana, 1996, p. 106.

> before us in English the force of everybody wanting and insisting on his rights, nobody thinking of his duty. And, where everybody wants rights, who shall give them to whom? I do not wish to imply that they do no duties. They don't perform the duties corresponding to those rights; and as they do not perform that particular duty, namely, acquire fitness, their rights have proved a burden to them.[37]

What Gandhi suggested was a political system achieved by means of duties and in balance with the spirit of truth. That is why he rejected the Machiavellian essence of modern politics and its demagogic end results. His appeal to the duties and responsibilities of the citizens, as the centre of self-governing politics, was based neither on a Manichaean friend–enemy distinction nor on the violent intervention of the masses. As a matter of fact, the Gandhian political revolution was beyond both common party politics and mobocracy.

Gandhian political revolution could be considered as the process of formation of individual self-realization as a vital component of political self-governance. He contended that an appeal to the moral conscience of the citizenry fortified and guaranteed the integral connection between truth and non-violence. Author Raghavan Iyer argued, 'Ahimsa is not a quality to be displayed to order, but an inward growth depending for sustenance upon intense individual effort, and it can be effectively taught only by living it. It is not a mere passive quality but the mightiest force man is

---

[37]Gandhi, M.K., *'Hind Swaraj' and Other Writings*, Anthony J. Parel (ed.), Cambridge University Press, Cambridge, 1997, pp. 81–2.

endowed with.'[38] Gandhi's appeal to the duty of the citizen was ultimately an appeal to the moral conscience of the individual in the pursuit of truth and non-violence.

In a sense, Gandhian political revolution started where violence ended. That is the reason why he always called the attention of his readers to the necessary relation between non-violence and swaraj. He observed:

> Swaraj does consist in the change of government and its real control by the people, but that would be merely the form. The substance that I am hankering after is a definite acceptance of the means and therefore a real change of heart on the part of the people... After all, self-government depends entirely upon our internal strength, upon our ability to fight against the heaviest odds. Indeed, self-government which does not require that continuous striving to attain it and to sustain it is not worth of name. I have therefore endeavoured to show both in word and deed, that political self-government, that is, self-government for a large number of men and women, is no better than individual self-government, and, therefore, it is to be attained precisely by the same means that the required for individual self-government or self-rule...[39]

For Gandhi, Swaraj was grounded in spiritual experience of truth, not in any form of political ideology. As a result,

---

[38]Iyer, Raghavan, *The Moral and Political Thought of Mahatma Gandhi*, Oxford University Press, New York, 1973, pp. 195–6.

[39]Gandhi, Mahatma, *Selected Political Writings*, Dennis Dalton (ed.), Hackett Publishing, Indiana, 1996, pp. 99–100.

he believed that a spiritual attitude in political life is indispensable for a well-functioning society. But he refused to think and act in terms of an ideal religious society where theology and politics went hand in hand. Rajmohan Gandhi put it correctly:

> Between a politics that pretended that religion was absent from India and a politics that squarely faced religion's hold, Gandhi chose the latter, and tried to remind all concerned that true Hinduism taught goodwill, and that true Islam, Sikhism and Christianity did the same. [...] without him intolerance would have been even stronger in both Hindu India and Muslim India.[40]

Gandhi faced neither religion nor a political ideology but only truth. He dealt respectfully and tolerantly with all religious groups and political movements in India. Maybe, that is why he stood out in the modern Indian intellectual and political life. The world has known Mahatma Gandhi as the prophet of non-violence in the twentieth century, but that is only one side of him. The other side was his struggle with his conscience, which he carried till death took him away. There is no reason to think that this struggle was a lost cause. A lost cause is one wherein we give up on our moral conscience and this never happened to Gandhi. As absurd as it may sound these days, one point seems certain in the Gandhian political revolution and that is the ethical foundation of all

---

[40]Gandhi, Rajmohan, *Mohandas: A True Story of a Man, His People and an Empire*, Penguin Books, New Delhi, 2006, p. 666.

political action. He never considered manipulation of power as a true political action. For him, politics worthy of the name was a matter of serving humanity. He always practised politics by thinking to lead by example. He tried to get his companions and collaborators to be better than they thought they could be. He, therefore, brought the concept of politics to bear decency and civility.

> Gandhi approached the task of establishing a public ethic not only by ceaseless preaching and advice in particular cases, but also by his own example and that of his immediate followers. His actions and deeds became anecdotal material for oral and written communication and for parables that could be recounted to those who would listen as well as those who could read.[41]

Gandhian politics is fundamentally a civil politics, mediated through empathy and interdependence. Thus, the Gandhian 'moment' of politics is a distinctive experience of civic action. It is the existential moment of individual reinvention and self-realization in which non-violence becomes emancipatory praxis. For him, political action that aimed to undo the legitimacy of existing institutions must also generate new modes of individual and collective self-rule to reconstitute and stabilize the political realm. For him, politics was essentially an ethical mode of conduct. Therefore, as a pluralist thinker and a practitioner of

[41]Rudolph, Lloyd I. and Susanne Hoeber Rudolph, 'The Private Origins of a Public Ethic: Gandhi and Civility', *Economic and Political Weekly*, 5 August 1967, Vol. 2, No. 31, p. 1381.

empathetic humanism, he found it necessary in approaching and understanding other cultures and religions. As such, the entire Gandhian thought in the realm of politics revolved around his critique of the epistemological arrogance of modernity and its authoritarian practices in terms of colonial thinking and imperialistic domination.

Gandhi was well aware of the fact that politics can lose its meaning when it turns into an instrument of power that takes away autonomy, maturity and self-mastery from human beings. He affirmed: 'Democracy is not a state in which people act like sheep. Under democracy, individual liberty of opinion and action is jealously guarded.'[42]

From Gandhi's point of view, democracy, as a constitutive element of swaraj, had to come from within. As a matter of fact, the recurrent theme in his thinking about democracy was the enlightened consciousness of the citizenry, which represented a defense against ignorance, prejudice, superstition and irresponsibility. Dalton said, 'If Gandhi's advocacy of democracy carries the warning to the government of a continuing sanction for mass civil disobedience, it also admonishes the citizenry of its collective responsibility.'[43] In other words, what Gandhi learned from party politics and disliked was that any political expertise that is not grounded in responsibility is dangerous and destructive. Sometimes people wrongly think that, in his handling of political affairs, Gandhi was too much of an idealist and dreamer. It should

---

[42]Fischer, Louis (ed.), *The Essential Gandhi | His Life, Work, and Ideas: An Anthology*, Vintage Books, New York, 1983, p. 192.

[43]Dalton, Dennis, *Gandhi: Nonviolent Power in Action*, Columbia University Press, New York, 1993, p. 78.

be pointed out that if India enjoys the respect it does in the world today, it is assuredly due to the level of decency and civility of the Gandhian political revolution. We were left with this moral direction of the political after Gandhi's assassination. It turned into a significant testament for the heritage of modern politics.

As such, one needs to endorse the relevance of Gandhian political revolution in present times through the key moments of non-violent political action in the American civil rights movement, the anti-apartheid movement in South Africa and finally in the Czechoslovakian resistance against communism. Furthermore, in the past 30 years, the world has consistently witnessed the 'Gandhian moment' of political non-violence in Serbia, Ukraine, Georgia, Myanmar, Hong Kong, Iran, Egypt and Tunisia. All these events and changes show us that it makes sense to talk about the general impact of the Gandhian political revolution in our contemporary world.

Let us be clear: when we lose touch with Gandhian politics, we inevitably lose the capacity to influence reality non-violently. The outcome of this process is familiar to us through all the political experiences mentioned above. The plain truth is that consistent moral and political recognitions of the 'Gandhian moment' of self-transformation found a common fate in the register of what we can call a 'global satyagraha'. Among these, Martin Luther King Jr's struggle for justice and equality for African Americans, which took place mainly in the 1950s and 1960s, placed before us an ethical mirror as powerful as that of Gandhi. The former's non-violent campaigns in Montgomery, Selma, Washington DC, Memphis and elsewhere were the exemplification of the influence of Gandhi's innovative revolution in the domain of politics and the demonstration of the fact that there could be no approach to political life without an appeal to the ethical. The Gandhian distinction between just and unjust laws benefited King's non-violent action by allowing it not only to be part of an effort to desegregate American society but also to think in terms of a more egalitarian democracy. As such, King considered non-violence a praxis of emancipation, and to be facilitating the capacity of living and acting together. This human interconnectedness, which avoids exclusion and humiliation, was described by King as an act of love that includes forgiveness and reconciliation. For King, as for Gandhi, love was an ethical act of transformation of social and political relationships in a society. As a result, King was convinced that politics was about creative self-organization of society and lifting men's eyes to the struggle for equality and justice. This struggle demanded suffering and self-sacrifice, something that lacked in the liberal organization of the world. He, therefore, argued:

> The Negro revolt is evolving into more than a quest for desegregation and equality. It is a challenge to a system that has created miracles of production and technology to create justice. If humanism is locked outside of the system, Negroes will have revealed its inner core of despotism and a far greater struggle for liberation will unfold.[44]

---

[44]King, Martin Luther, Jr, *Conscience for Change: Massey Lectures*, Seventh Series, Canadian Broadcasting Corporation, Toronto, 1967, pp. 9–10.

Going back to the Gandhian political revolution, we can say that swaraj, as Gandhi understood it, with Martin Luther King Jr following the same path, was both a work of political emancipation and an act of love. Gandhi made a compelling case for the power of love in order to transform collective consciousness against injustice and unethical politics.

As such, he was trying to forcefully challenge the mainstream political ideas on sovereignty. Gandhian political revolution was the inversion of modern political theory as a philosophy of individual rights and modern state into a theory of interdependent citizenship and non-violent action. His theory of politicized love helped him transcend the Hobbesian approach to politics as a universal desire for self-preservation. Gandhi essentially replaced the Hobbesian security paradigm of politics, which raises the question of the state as a political agent responsible for implementing the requirements of human security, with his own paradigm of politicized love and human solidarity. Accordingly, Gandhi's project of empathetic emancipation through non-violent action had the twin objectives of bringing about a truly democratic transformation of society, and thereby securing an ethical social order for the individual and the community. Empathy, for Gandhi, was the search for what was ethical. It was a way of transforming an enemy into a companion and an ally. 'When love is bestowed on the so-called enemy, it is tested, it becomes a virtue... Love can fight; often, it is obliged to.'[45] For Gandhi, the concept of politicized

[45]Gandhi, Mahatma, *Selected Political Writings*, Dennis Dalton (ed.), Hackett Publishing, Indiana, 1996, pp. 55–6.

love suggested the existence of an empathetic community, which transcends the cold and faceless utilitarian legality and sovereignty. Therefore, the concept of politicized love pointed to the existence of the political subject as a member of a common humanity.

Mandela's reading of Mahatma Gandhi and his political construction of the 'Gandhian moment' in South African politics was also an exemplification of the 'ethicalization of politics'. Mandela considered mutual toleration between the white and black South Africans as a golden rule of political conduct. He analysed the essential unity of humanity as the process of recognition of the other, necessitating critical self-examination and a move from egoistic centricity towards a shared humanity. For him, as was for Gandhi, non-violence was a transformative ontological and political project, geared towards a kaleidoscopic view of society and the world. Moving beyond fear allowed Mandela, as a political subject, to move beyond the sovereignty of an unjust state that created violence. Following Gandhi, he came to the conclusion that the political subject was not the consequence of a centralized state sovereignty and rather state sovereignty was to be considered as the outcome of the interdependence of political subjects. For Mandela, as was for Gandhi, the problem of politics was not just to answer the question of 'Who rules?' but also to respond to the question of 'What are the conditions of a shared sovereignty?' It was with this Gandhian spirit in mind that Mandela accepted to join hands with his enemies in order to drag South Africa out of hatred and bloodshed. He affirmed: 'All South Africans must now unite and join hands and say we are one country, one nation, one people, marching together into the future.'[46]

Last but not least, one of the most important outcomes of Gandhian political revolution was seen in the thoughts of Václav Havel and in his central role as a dissident intellectual and civic actor in the Velvet Revolution (Sametová Revoluce) of 1989 in Czechoslovakia. It entailed a non-violent transition of power. Though very European in essence, it is undeniable that the democratic movement envisaged by Havel and other Czech and Slovak civic actors was born out of a Gandhian idea of 'ethicalization of politics'. The Velvet Revolution embraced the Gandhian ethics of empathy and his commitment to human dignity, while insisting on the idea of speaking the truth as the right moral and political alternative to totalitarianism. Havel's attitude towards non-violent construction of the new Czech society was based on the two Gandhian ideas of 'living in truth' and adhering to a 'higher responsibility'. Havel wrote:

> When I speak of living within truth, I naturally do not have in mind only products of conceptual thought, such as a protest or a letter written by a group of intellectuals. It can be any means by which a person or a group revolts against manipulation: anything from a letter by intellectuals to a workers' strike, from a rock concert to a student demonstration, from refusing to vote in the farcical elections, to making an open speech

[46]Hain, Peter, *Mandela: His Essential Life*, Rowman & Littlefield, London, 2018, p. 149.

> at some official congress, or even a hunger strike, for instance. If the suppression of the aims of life is a complex process, and if it is based on the multifaceted manipulation of all expressions of life then, by the same token, every free expression of life indirectly threatens the post-totalitarian system politically, including forms of expression to which, in other social systems, no one would attribute any potential political significance, not to mention explosive power.[47]

If for Gandhi, experiments with politics had a fundamental and ethical premise in finding major exemplifications in the values of responsibility, civility and tolerance, for Havel, too, political action was marked by notions such as 'truth' and 'conscience'.

In the light of the global impact of Gandhian political revolution, it makes sense to underline that for Gandhi, politics worthy of the name is the one that strives for decency, responsibility, civility, sincerity and truth-seeking. His vision of politics, therefore, was premised on an understanding of the crucial ethics of citizenship in the making of the everydayness of politics.

When Gandhi criticized his fellow Congressmen of not being in touch with the Indian masses, he was defining politics not as the rule of the party oligarch but as a sovereignty shared by everyone, including the misfits and the pariahs. He wrote:

---

[47]Havel, Václav, et al., 'The Power of the Powerless', *The Power of the Powerless: Citizens Against the State in Central-Eastern Europe*, Routledge, London, 1985, p. 43.

> The Congress must progressively represent the masses. They are as yet untouched by politics. They have no political consciousness of the type our politicians desire. Their politics are confined to bread and salt. I dare not say butter, for millions do not know the taste of ghee or even oil. Their politics are confined to communal adjustments. It is right however to say that we the politicians do represent the masses in opposition to the government. But if we begin to use them before they are ready, we shall cease to represent them. We must first come in living touch with them by working for them and in their midst. We must share their sorrows, understand their difficulties and anticipate their wants. With the pariahs we must be pariahs and see how we feel to clean the closets of the upper classes and have the remains of their table thrown at us. We must see how we like being in the boxes, miscalled houses, of the labourers of Bombay. We must identify ourselves with the villagers who toil under the hot sun beating on their bent backs and see how we would like to drink water from the pool in which the villagers bathe, wash their clothes and pots and in which their cattle drink and roll. Then and not till then shall we truly represent the masses and they will, as surely as I am writing this, respond to every call.[48]

---

[48]Gandhi, Mahatma, *Selected Political Writings*, Dennis Dalton (ed.), Hackett Publishing, Indiana, 1996, p. 143.

We can conclude that the Gandhian political revolution is a way of seeing the world from below. This is how Gandhi escaped and opposed all elitism and bureaucratization of party politics. He never got involved with what Havel called the 'peculiar dialectical dance of truths and lies' of party politics.[49] He was a witness to the rise and fall of liberal democracies, but ultimately, he knew well that citizen maturity is the primary condition of democracy. For Gandhi, the plain truth was that we can talk seriously about democracy and politics in real sense of the terms, which involves participation in the making of political institutions. Having said that, we can understand the relevance of the Gandhian political revolution in relation to the political challenges of today's world.

In short, Gandhi's appeal for the notions of self-governance, higher responsibility, truth-seeking and shared sovereignty is an invitation to a new political experience in the twenty-first century. If we realize this, then we must also bear in mind that all the global challenges that we face today are interrelated. Gandhi based his political revolution on a moral one, but he knew well that politics is the art of the possible, only and only if we can improve ourselves by understanding better and forming a deeper interconnectedness with the surrounding world and the natural environment. He evaluated his task in the following terms: 'My goal is friendship with the whole world and I can combine the greatest love with the greatest opposition

---

[49]Tucker, Scott, 'Our Queer World: Capitalism with a Human Face?' *The Humanist*, Vol. 54, No. 3, May/June 1994, pp. 40–2.

to wrong.'[50] Gandhi was hopeful that there would come a day when humanity would return to that beautiful word: peace.

[50]Kripalani, Krishna (ed.), *All Men are Brothers*, Navajivan Publishing House, Ahmedabad, 1960, p. 156.

THREE

Gandhian Economic Revolution

Gandhian moral revolution, self-transformation of the individual and society impact the ethical revolution in politics. Having understood the significance of ethical revolution, this chapter characterizes Gandhian revolution in the way society perceives economics and economic systems. History has witnessed not only the uniformity of crises and challenges across the globe but also similar responses from the human race spread across the regions. This reinforces the spiritual connectivity of humans indeed.

Having explored one's self or consciousness and discovered the unfathomed mystery of truth, an individual seeks to dwell in a world comprising non-violent and peaceful socio-economic settings. The Gandhian perspective on economics emerges from the primary dimensions of upliftment and enrichment of human life. The underlying motivation is not to attain a higher standard of living, but to achieve at least minimal possible respect for human and social values. Gandhian economics is guided by an evolved consciousness that realizes the truth of existence and, therefore, seeks ultimate satisfaction. Guided by empathy and the law of non-possession, its ultimate aim is to build a society that is devoid of any concentration of power, competition, warfare and unrest. Consumerism is by no way a method to achieve individual satisfaction.

The underlying phenomenon that 'human wants are unlimited but resources are limited' constitutes the basic economic problem: the problem of scarcity. In this context, the philosophical approach of the Gandhian economic perspective strategically distinguishes between the notion of wants and desires, and provides a necessary rationale behind ethical wants. Thus, the basic economic problem 'of scarcity and choice' describes the explanations in the Gandhian notion of economics.

It is evident that the desire to acquire more and more has been detrimental to the limited resources, and has ultimately administered unprecedented possession of resources. The outcome of greed has been unchecked capitalism that breeds more and more economic growth. Thus, one can conveniently state that the uncontrolled and unlimited human wants have resulted in the concentration of wealth in the hands of a few. The dynamics of political economy further plays a critical role in disrupting equity in the distribution and the existence of the welfare state.

The 'invisible hands' of profits or forces of demand and supply were responsible for capitalism to grow uncontrolled and detrimental to the extent of destroying human values and ethics.[51] Moreover, the Keynesian notion—increasing demand could lead to a multiplier effect and distribute growth among the poorest of the poor—has subsequently

---

[51]Smith, Adam, *The Essential Adam Smith*, W.W. Norton & Company, 1987.

failed. In addition, the political economy, guided by vested interests, interrupts the flow of well-being to every section of society. Economist Pulin B. Nayak concluded that its prospects and long-run viability are delimited by ecological imbalance and growing inequalities associated with it.[52] The two well-known economists Lucas Chancel and Thomas Piketty also revealed that from 1980 to 2014, the gap between the rich and the poor had aggravated in India.[53] The purpose of development must be to converge and reduce the inequality levels prevailing in the economies. However, the extensive literature on growth theories explicitly reveals that the rich are becoming more affluent and the poor are becoming poorer, which is increasing inequalities.[54]

In all development debates, 'regional inequality' has been ignored. The existence of high-income inequality challenges the basic argument of Robert M. Solow's growth theory, which advocates that competitive forces and inter-regional migration will allow regional inequality

[52]Nayak, Pulin B., 'Present Crises of Capitalism and Its Reforms', *Economic and Political Weekly*, Vol. 55, No. 17, 2020.

[53]Chancel, Lucas and Thomas Piketty, 'Indian Income Inequality, 1922–2015: From British Raj to Billionaire Raj?' *The Review of Income and Wealth*, Series 65, No. S1, November 2019, pp. S33–S62, https://bit.ly/3NRmhvX. Accessed on 8 July 2022.

[54]Chandrasekhar, C.P. and Jayati Ghosh, 'Recent Employment Trends in India and China: An Unfortunate Convergence?', *Social Scientist*, Vol. 35, No. 3/4, 2007, pp. 19–46; Sengupta, Manimay, 'Unemployment Duration and the Measurement of Unemployment,' *The Journal of Economic Inequality*, Vol. 7, No. 3, 2008, pp. 273–94.

to disappear through gradual factor price equalization.[55] The famous Kuznets curve advocated an inverted U-shaped curve, postulating that inequality first increases and then decreases over time.[56] William J. Baumol[57] and Robert J. Barro[58] determined convergence in developed countries and divergence in less-developed nations.

Under the prevailing economic system, humans are caught under the vicious cycle of consumerism. The characteristics of greed, vested interest and preponderance of power have become the basic nature of humankind. Such adverse human attributes lead humanity towards destruction, unrest, conflicts and war. The failure of economic development to ensure inclusive growth, poverty alleviation and reduction in inequality makes it imperative to revisit the prevailing models of growth and development. Moreover, economics devoid of ethics is destructive, barbarous and environmentally detrimental.

Gandhian economic thought originates from the perspective of an individual self. All wants and desires, both materialistic and non-materialistic, emerge from one's self. These desires and unlimited wants constitute the demand

---

[55]Solow, Robert M., *Growth Theory: An Exposition*, Oxford University Press, New York, 2000.

[56]Kuznets, Simon, 'Economic Growth and Income Inequality', *The American Economic Review*, Vol. XLV, No. 1, 1955, https://bityl.co/Dccq. Accessed on 8 July 2022.

[57]Baumol, William J., 'Productivity Growth, Convergence, and Welfare: What the Long-Run Data Show', *The American Economic Review*, Vol. 76, No. 5, 1986, pp. 1072–85.

[58]Barro, Robert J., 'Economic Growth in a Cross Section of Countries', *The Quarterly Journal of Economics*, Vol. 106, No. 2, 1991, pp. 407–43.

side of economics. Consequently, an evolved self that is guided by the wisdom of Gandhian thoughts will aim for self-sufficiency, self-reliance and minimum consumption. Moreover, the interconnectivity of the self of each individual and finally to the larger consciousness should become the guiding force for economic decisions and choices for the economy as a whole.

Every dimension of human life, such as politics, economics, socio-economic systems and the sociocultural and ecological dimension, must originate from the interconnectivity between every individual and the larger consciousness. When any of these dimensions of human life loses its connection with the individual self, it results in imbalance and loss of harmony. Against this backdrop, when the economic system operates with the profit motive to attain material well-being, the welfare of the people in the society comes to be ignored and compromised.

Humans' welfare exists in happiness and peace. Therefore, the ethical aim of every economic system must be to attain happiness, sociological and psychological well-being, and ultimately sustain human dignity. When individuals are guided by spiritual enquiry and ethical value judgement, the desires and wants are transformed into minimal material needs for sustaining a simple living. The purpose of the economy is to attain the welfare of the community. It is the State's ethical responsibility to ensure human dignity and eliminate inequalities of ownership and income. Finally, all economic systems must intend to attain inclusivity and economic equality by narrowing the class gap in society.

The Gandhian notion of 'economy of permanence' proposed by J.C. Kumarappa provides sufficient explanation on the issue of supply, which is constrained by limited resources.[59] Thriving on the concepts of stock and flow, the economy of permanence depicts sustainable pathways of production and consumption. The attributes of self-sufficiency and self-reliance envisage that the individuals should be satisfied with minimum consumption. Such a society is devoid of concentration of power, competition, warfare and unrest.

The two fundamental notions of Gandhi, namely 'the Gandhian trusteeship model' and economy of permanence, are considered as benchmarks for revolutionizing both economic and environmental domains. The rules of the game in economics have to be redefined and revisited. We need to unlearn and redefine its fundamentals. If we want to visualize sustainability and regain the lost harmony with nature, the definition of economics has to evolve from the individual self to society, and then finally to the State. All three entities—individuals, firms and the State—have to function in the same direction with the same objective. This will then lead to the origination of a socio-economic transformation, which will be referred to as Gandhian economic revolution. It is only then that we will be able to visualize a climate-resilient society, which would ensure a better place to live for our future generations.

The Gandhian ideology of trusteeship is a remarkable

[59]Kumarappa, J.C., *Gandhian Economic Thought*, Sarva Seva Sangh Prakashan, 2010.

breakthrough in economic thought, unfolding the dilemma of the economic problem of unlimited wants and limited means. The trusteeship philosophy is based on the notion, 'One must care about a world one will not see.' Much before the climate change debate began, Gandhi had said that we should act as 'trustees' and use natural resources wisely as it is our moral responsibility to ensure that we bequeath to the future generations a healthy planet. The Gandhian perceptive of economics emerges from the primary dimensions or aspects of development emphasized by him. These aspects are mainly upliftment and enrichment of human life, rather than a higher standard of living. The key driving force behind the Gandhian economic thought is the availability of at least the minimal possible respect for social values. In his philosophy, ethical values dominate economic values.

A unique character of non-possession is imparted through the concept of the trusteeship model—a model that advocates refraining from possession of any sort. The doctrine of trusteeship guarantees human dignity to all. In addition, it creates empathy among all humans in society, connecting them to not only one another but the entire ecosystem. The perception of ownership or possession is detrimental to peace and harmony. Possession promotes greed, selfish interest and accumulation. A State that adopts the notion of trusteeship is devoid of possession and embraces all living and non-living material as its custodian and guards their safety. Exploitation is non-existent in trusteeship because there is no incentive to accumulate or any scope of selfish interest. Self-sacrifice and selfless services become the two characteristics of the State, all organizations and stakeholders. These remarkable attributes then cultivate sustainable development and growth.

The trusteeship model and economy of permanence, advocated by Gandhian thoughts, transform the way humans envisage their interaction with nature and perceive their existence on earth. This encourages humans to respect the continuity of life. The genesis of Gandhian economics evolves with the individual's self, then goes on to society and finally the State. The role of individuals, firms and the State are aligned in one direction—to serve humanity and its ethical existence. With this, a Gandhian economic revolution sets in.

The discipline of economics deals with the problem of scarcity through the theory of economic growth and development. The Gandhian concept of the trusteeship model unfolds the dilemma of the problem of scarcity by proposing the most efficient way of treating surplus in an economy. Guided by the fundamentals of ethical economics and human upliftment, the spirit of trusteeship doctrine emerges from the law of non-possession. The thought advocates that the bounties of the world are primarily for the entire human race as a whole and not for any particular individual alone. When an individual processes more than what is rationally needed, he has the ethical responsibility to distribute.

> Supposing I have come by a fair amount of wealth—either by way of legacy or by means of trade and industry—I must know that all that wealth does not belong to me; what belongs to me is the right to an honourable livelihood, no better than that enjoyed by

> millions of others. The rest of my wealth belongs to the community and must be used for the welfare of the community.[60]

According to Gandhi's trusteeship principle, when some people work and earn more, their surplus wealth should be used for the welfare of the poor and those less privileged. The trusteeship model advocated by him essentially uplifts the economic order of society to an egalitarian one. The core of the trusteeship model is the protection of human dignity and not merely material prosperity. Under the state-regulated trusteeship, individuals will not be free to hold or use wealth for selfish satisfaction and disregard the interest of society. Such a system will ensure a minimum wage for all the members of society. Besides, this doctrine of trusteeship addresses the prevailing inequalities of ownership and income, narrowing the class gap in society.[61]

An economic system that adopts the Gandhian trusteeship model can comprehend the need and plight of every human being that is living within its boundaries or territory. The government acts as a trustee or custodian of resources and intends to distribute its resources equitably to all living within its boundaries; no one owns or consumes excess resources, and all resources that are in excess are distributed among the people who are deprived and in need. The trusteeship notion communicates the attributes of empathy and non-

---

[60]*Harijan*, 23 February 1947.

[61]Kesavulu, Y., 'Gandhian Trusteeship as an "Instrument of Human Dignity"', *Gandhi Marg,* vol. 25, No. 4, January–March 2004, https://bit.ly/3bYE4nN. Accessed on 8 July 2022.

possession. Humans are custodians of all natural and man-made capital. This elementary character of non-possession is devoid of greed, selfishness and competition. Thus, the policymakers, the decision-makers as well as individuals perform their respective roles with an empathic attitude, which is extremely needed in present times.

The elementary aspects of the Gandhian notion of self-sufficiency and self-reliance envisage that individuals feel satisfied with minimum consumption. Such a society or community would be devoid of any concentration of power, competition, warfare and unrest. Nations comprising such societies or communities would be peaceful, non-violent and have equitable distribution of wealth. Resources should be produced and consumed sustainably keeping such an economic set-up or regime in mind.

Although the doctrine of the welfare state was developed around the 1990s, economists soon realized the missing concept of human welfare while discussing the mechanism of economics. Several noted welfare economists, such as Kenneth J. Arrow[62], attempted to integrate social welfare and the concept of utility. The Benthamite notion contended that 'it is the greatest happiness of the greatest number that is the measure of right and wrong'.[63] Later, the Rawlsian approach measured the well-being of the worst-off individual.[64]

---

[62]Arrow, Kenneth J., 'A Difficulty in the Concept of Social Welfare', *The Journal of Political Economy*, Vol. 58. No. 4, 1950, pp. 328–46.

[63]Burns, J.H., and Hart H.L.A. (ed.), *A Comment on the Commentaries and A Fragment on Government (The Collected Works of Jeremy Bentham)*, Clarendon Press, 2008.

[64]Rawls, John, *A Theory of Justice*, Harvard University Press, 1971.

John Rawls asserted that equal fundamental liberties are to be embodied in the political constitution, and that they relate to fair equality of opportunity and general benefit of the least advantaged members of society.

Though welfare economics attempted to incorporate some of the human ethics and value judgement, there has been no evidence or testimony of implementation of the notion of welfare economics. Certain countries, like Norway, Canada, etc., have attempted to implement such a welfare model. However, the critical aspect of the State being the custodian of nature has not been enforced.

An economy based on the notion of economy of permanence plays an instrumental role in ensuring sustainable growth. In Kumarappa's remarkable work, *Economy of Permanence,* much emphasis is laid on sustainable economy, which finds its foundation in the Gandhian pathway of truth and non-violence. The notion of economy of permanence advocates the choice of resources that are non-exhaustible or permanent. An economy based on the philosophy of Kumarappa is not only environmentally sustainable but can also achieve sustainable growth.

The notion of an economy of permanence thrives on the concept of stock and flow. A transient and permanent economy depicts the sustainable pathways of production and consumption. Nature, however, is considered permanent in comparison to human life, which is transient. Since man consumes nature and its resources for his survival and existence, Kumarappa proposes that an economy that relies more on the permanent elements of nature, as compared to the stock, will ultimately be more sustainable. Kumarappa asserts, 'Everything begins somewhere and ceases to exist sometime.'[65]

The Gandhian philosophy of interconnectedness between means and ends as described in Chapter 1 can also be applied in economics. 'They say "means are after all means." I would say "means are after all everything". As the means so the end."'[66] In economics, means are the resources or inputs that are utilized to meet the ends or demands. The role of means is critical for a permanent economy that attempts to sustain the continuity of life in the environment. The means to fulfil minimal material needs must be ethical and environmentally viable.

As discussed before, individual actors have the power to change history, and therefore, should be questioned and held responsible when the freedom of the people at large is destroyed. This principle also holds economic validity as individual wants and desires constitute the foundation of the economy. An individual is responsible for creating demand in the economy and is equally responsible for its subsequent impact on the environment.

When individuals in an economy are driven by profits and material well-being, ethical values and human well-being take a back seat. Material well-being can never be equitable because it thrives on greed and unprecedented accumulation of wealth and capital. Subjugation and preponderance of power are the instincts of material accumulation.

---

[65]Kumarappa, J.C., *Gandhian Economic Thought*, Sarva Seva Sangh Prakashan, 1951.

[66]Kripalani, Krishna (ed.), *All Men are Brothers*, Navajivan Publishing House, Ahmedabad, 1960, p. 134.

Consequently, the State that controls the economy under such an unethical and uncontrolled value system is capsized by the harmful consequences of the political economy. Thus, it is almost impossible to visualize equity in the distribution of wealth and resources when political economy takes the centre stage in distribution. The entire power of distribution becomes unjust and skewed and caters to the needs of a particular section of society, depriving many of the benefits of growth and development.

The role of the State is extremely significant. It must be motivated to serve humanity. Service to humankind and custodianship of natural resources must be the two indispensable commitments of the State. When a community, nation or State is based on the Gandhian philosophy of truth and non-violence, then the system of governance is based on human service and human resource development. The element of human service should never be decoupled from the gross element of human development. The latter alone leads to destruction and is associated with an increase in ecological footprint. When the core purpose of governance is human service, then the socio-economic order that is produced becomes peaceful and sustainable.

In this context, a decentralized system of governance then takes the centre stage. Under this, the village panchayat, the primary political unit of public administration, is seen as self-governing, self-sufficient and autonomous. When small communities decide the best optimal allocation of every provision on consensus-based choices, then there is no unrest. They take up complete responsibility for providing goods and services, subject to availability of resources and capabilities.

A decentralized, consensus-based, decision-making system is another significant aspect of Gandhian philosophy. Such decentralized communities are characterized as self-reliant and self-sufficient. These communities are more non-violent and sustainable, reflecting lesser exploitation of resources; they are more peaceful and ecologically sustainable.

Centralized and decentralized systems are the two instruments prescribed for bringing about socio-economic benefits to an economy. Like any other system their objectives are well defined in not only creating wealth as efficiently as possible but also distributing it widely and evenly. A centralized setting, however, is highly vulnerable to being trapped in the clutches of the political economy, depriving a large population living in remote areas from achieving basic facilities. A system should be inclusive and conducive to the peace and harmony of society.

The quest for power, implying a desire to possess all materials and resources, is associated with violence. Power comes through wealth and the desire to rule, exhibiting superiority over others. A centralized method of production generates an accumulation of capital, leading to the concentration of wealth. The concentration of economic wealth implies competition leading to violence, and consequently, maintaining hegemony and supremacy over others. Therefore, the need to expand based on greed instigates more and more of competitive environment, leading to over-exploitation of resources and overproduction.

Large-scale production demands an increase in the accumulation of raw material and, hence, encourages warfare. Thus, the need to find markets for finished products would ultimately lead to imperialism. Neag Mihai-Marcel, Halmaghi Elisabeta-Emilia and Cucuiet Mâţu Petruţa argue that globalization and the emergence of international markets increase the need for nations to adopt an integrated approach for policy formulation considering both internal or domestic policies as well as external cooperation, since global economies are highly dependent on each other.[67] Finally, globalization has instigated cooperation and competition for power and proven hegemony over resources and markets.

In the face of scarcity of capital, a decentralized system of governance is the only plausible option. Further, in the case of excess labour, unemployment and underemployment, centralization is aggravating the problems all the more. The alternative would be the best way of producing goods when raw materials and markets are in the proximity of producing centres. This system would lead to a far more equal distribution of wealth and also make people tolerant. This process of production would include the distribution of wealth in a more equitable manner. It would be a consensus-based system, where every individual would matter in making any socio-economic policy or decision. Thus, a decentralized setting would empower each producer and make him an entrepreneur, improving his standard of living, further uplifting the average intelligence of the nation as a whole.

---

[67]Neag, Mihai-Marcel, et al., 'Contributions on the Determination of the Relationship among Globalization, Sustainable Development and Energy Security', *Scientific Bulletin*, Vol. 22, No. 1, 2017, pp. 24–30.

In a decentralized framework, there will be no disturbance of peace at the nationwide level. Moreover, where small producers are working in a decentralized setting, the raw material required for production will be exploited only locally. The system will not entail exercising its power over the raw materials. Supply demands will be met without the use of violence. Such an economy will not provide any opportunity for a wealthy person at the cost of less fortunate others. This will further inculcate human values among those living in the society. Effectively speaking, a sense of human values will direct economic activities and drive away various negativities in the global environment—international rivalry, jealousy and competition will be minimized, leading to human progress, peace and prosperity.

The elementary aspects of the Gandhian notion of self-sufficiency and self-reliance envisage that individuals be satisfied with minimum consumption. A society or community that follows this notion would be devoid of any concentration of power, competition, warfare and unrest. Such nations would be peaceful and non-violent, with equitable distribution of wealth. Provided there is such an economic set-up or regime, the resources of the economy must be produced and consumed sustainably.

Numerous examples can be used here to illustrate the success stories of anti-globalization and protectionism. Cuba's economy survived decently after the US embargo in 1960. Another example is the functioning of Mendha, a small village of Gonda tribals in central India. It is under the Dhanora tehsil of the Gadchiroli district in the state of Maharashtra. Though it is very much in contact with the outside world, it has maintained its unique characteristics, like the non-existence of disputes and difference of opinions; there is no problem of poverty, hunger, unemployment and economic disparities. The village functions are effectively based on the unanimous decision of the village community. A village assembly called *gaon samaj sabha*, comprising all adult members of the village, takes the critical decisions. In one of the meetings of the village assembly, it was decided to impose a ₹150-fine on the cutting of trees in the forest for fruits, leaves and branches or even honey. The villagers, even today, depend on forests for food and fuel, and use biogas as a source of energy. This village serves as a remarkable example of people's power of forming collective consensus when it comes to decision-making.[68]

A decentralized community formed on a consensus-based decision-making system will provide social capital for economic growth and development, and will be defined by an ethical and moral value system. Let us comprehend how moral revolution and self-rule will help shape social capital which, in turn, embarks the ethical revolution in economics.

The journey of moral revolution is not confined to individuals only. As discussed in Chapter 2, the Gandhian moral revolution transformed the entire relation between the definition of civilization and the architecture of ethics. In addition, self-governance as a model for the entire nation is plausible only if every individual becomes truthful and undergoes a suitable degree of self-transformation as illustrated in Chapter 3. Self-rule can be conceived through a

---

[68]Tofa, D.N. and M.H. Hiralal, *Menda (Lekha)*, Vrikshamitra, 2010.

decentralized system, provided each individual understands the ethical responsibility of his or everyone's actions and the consequent impact on socio-economic well-being of society.

A newly emerged concept of 'social capital', defined by the Organisation for Economic Co-operation and Development (OECD) in 1916, refers to 'networks together with shared norms, values and understandings that facilitate co-operation within or among groups'.[69] The certain value system and ethics that are engendered in such social groups are responsible for maintaining an individual's respect and security. When we address the notion of ethical economics, social capital serves as a significant asset for inclusive growth and development based on ethical value judgement. However, it is plausible that such a concept of social capital could result in the marginalization of a certain section of society that does not belong to the social capital.

It is only when Gandhian moral revolution and self-rule manifest that social capital serves as a crucial ingredient for economic growth, driven by ethics and value judgment. The entire purpose of augmenting ethics in economics is to offset the detrimental effect of capitalism, accumulation and political economy. Comprehending an economic model based on a decentralized system with social capital as a fundamental input will constitute an economy that is inclusive, sustainable and ethical. Such a system can be visualized on the basis of on self-rule and moral revolution.

An economic system that operates on the doctrine of

---

[69]Healy, Tom, 'The Measurement of Social Capital at International Level', *Social Capital: The Challenge of International Measurement Series,* https://bit.ly/3Paa7PC. Accessed on 8 July 2022.

trusteeship and adopts a sustainable economic model of an economy of permanence, based on social capital input, is far more inclusive, equitable and sustainable. Technology is the only concern or threat to its stability. Unprecedented technological breakthrough has become a serious concern of the present world. Let us now deliberate on how technology and technological breakthrough can be assimilated in the framework of Gandhian economics.

There is no conflict in the consensus that technology is the biggest threat not only to nature but also humankind. Technology depletes natural resources and is harmful to the environment. Technological breakthrough has been unprecedented and uncontrolled. Technology does not possess self-limiting principles and the virtues of self-balancing, self-adjusting and self-cleansing.[70] Consequently, economic growth driven by technological breakthrough is self-destructing and environmentally unsustainable. This provides a necessary rationale behind realizing the significance of ethics in the use of technology. A technology or a technological breakthrough that serves humanity and safeguards human values and ethics could be a part of ethical revolution.

The only mechanism that can control unprecedented evolution of technology is adhering to certain principles or ethics. Here, the ethics, which provide ultimate satisfaction from work, should be the objective. Modern technology eliminates the skilful and productive work of human hands. Thus, in modern technology, a person is deprived of the

---

[70]Schumacher, E.F., *Small Is Beautiful: A Study of Economics as if People Mattered*, Random House, 1993, p. 120.

kind of work he enjoys the most—one involving his hands, brain and natural talent.[71]

Related to this, Karl Marx wrote: 'It wishes to see only "useful things" produced, but it forgets that production of too many useful things produces too large a useless population.'[72] Technology not only disrupts the relationship maintained between humans and nature but also takes away human values, such as empathy, emotions and compassion. It impairs their connection with a value system and with their spiritual self. Gandhiji said, 'The poor of the world cannot be helped by mass production, only by production by the masses.'[73]

The system of mass production, based on sophisticated, highly capital-intensive, energy-intensive and labour-saving technology, is driven by cheap labour and capital accumulation. Sinful characteristics, such as greed and vested interests, are associated with large-scale production, which has nothing to do with the weaker and poorest section of society.[74] However, the concept of technology that is produced by the masses, indicates employment, economic liberty and self-rule for all.[75] At the same time, the masses mobilize their natural talent and creative art. It is unique and empowers local communities. Thus, the

---

[71]Ibid. 122.

[72]Marx, Karl, *Economic and Philosophical Manuscripts of 1844*, Progress Publishers, Moscow, 1959.

[73]Schumacher, E.F., *Small Is Beautiful: A Study of Economics as if People Mattered*, Random House, 1993, p. 126.

[74]Ibid. 127.

[75]Ibid. 126.

choice of technology adopted by a large number of people for production is one that is confined to the localized and community level, creating a decentralized setting, which is more compatible with laws of ecology. This leads to a smaller ecological footprint in the form of lesser use of resources.

Digitalization as an innovative technology can be perceived as a technological breakthrough, which might reduce consumerism. A lot of records are placed online, leading to lesser use of paper and minimal use of transportation. However, digitalization is bound to lead to more energy consumption unless it operates by deploying renewable energy sources. It is also accompanied by several fallouts that inhibit spiritual upliftment. Though it symbolizes more social connections, it is a considerable departure from the human value system. There is no ambiguity in stating that no matter how much social media advances or our connectivity with the world around us improves, such digitalization and use of technology is highly detrimental to individual freedom.

There is an urgent need for the State to take charge and control the negative fallouts of digitalization by safeguarding individual freedom. Institutionalizing the ethical norms of social media and digitalization through the legal framework by incorporating individuals from a community for their consensus is one of the remarkable recommendations originating from the Gandhian perspective.

Finally, to conclude, humanity is facing the most challenging times of this era. The unprecedented health disasters, natural calamities and socio-economic challenges, such as income inequalities, unemployment, etc., are some of the deep-rooted prevailing issues of the present times. In addition, the global issue of climate change has aggravated these challenges phenomenally. The prevailing socio-economic systems have found themselves incapable of resolving the vicious cycle of these challenges.

The unprecedented advent of the Covid-19 pandemic has made it extremely essential for all countries, regions and states to be self-reliant and self-sufficient. Each system and each region must be capable enough to manage their requirement of resources. Self-sufficiency will not only strengthen a nation, making it more resilient towards health risks, but also ensure a sustainable economy.[76] In addition, the emerging concerns of war and civil unrest make it imperative for nations to achieve self-sufficiency to encounter such health-related, unforeseen and unfortunate geopolitical emergencies. This is evident from the war in Ukraine, where there is a need for self-sufficiency and self-reliance, especially in the context of fuel dependency. Therefore, for a sustainable and resilient economy, becoming self-reliant and self-sufficient is necessary. The decentralized framework, as advocated by Gandhi, is self-reliant, self-sufficient and ensures sustainability.

All the present global challenges, such as climate change, natural disasters and pandemics, have been a result of the unprecedented outbreak of consumerism. A decentralized system will ensure minimum consumption, limited exploitation of resources, abatement of greed and excessive production and consumption. Within a decentralized system, overproduction and excessive consumerism are undesirable

---

[76]Alam, A., et al., 'A Review of Resource Management and Self-Reliance for Sustainable Development of India under Covid-19 Scenario', *Journal of Public Affairs,* Vol. 21, No. 4, 2021, p. e2725.

and avoided, which, in turn, can help resolve all the current issues and challenges associated with consumerism.

Earlier, due to the lack of application of science and technology, the need for spiritual enhancement was not as direly felt as it is in today's world. The spiritual experiments were limited to individual experiences. But today, it is the need of society at large. The discourse on spirituality is most essential in the present narratives of social interactions and norms. An apolitical, non-religious and unbiased mechanism is needed to save humanity and human values from the unprecedented technological breakthrough and transition.

Finally, the biggest global challenge of climate change finds its direct linkage with the use of conventional energy sources and unchecked economic growth. Gandhian thoughts illuminate and revolutionize the role of energy, while confronting the challenges posed by climate change.

FOUR

Gandhian Ecological Revolution

The Gandhian economic revolution is guided by an evolved consciousness that realizes the truth of existence and, therefore, seeks ultimate satisfaction. Guided by empathy and the law of non-possession, its ultimate aim is to build a society that is devoid of any concentration of power, competition, warfare and unrest.

Originating from evolved consciousness, humans possess the ability to connect their existence with nature. The unique feature of the equality and inclusivity of Gandhian thoughts is not only limited to humankind but extends to other living creatures and the environment. Gandhi's exemplar persistence with respect to the 'other' refers to nature, spiritual harmony and equilibrium between humankind and ecology.

Our material desires and wants accentuate the need for economic growth which, in turn, has a detrimental impact on the environment, leading to climate change. The dilemma of human activity and preserving natural resources has been persistent ever since human civilization came into existence. The Gandhian ideology of truth and love is not only limited to individual upliftment and enhancement but augments 'otherness of the other' and the interconnectedness between humankind and ecology.

The Gandhian paradigm is a spiritual endeavour that transforms every individual, thus, uplifting the spiritual existence through achieving higher consciousness. In this phenomenon of transformation, three primary connections are critical. First is the transformation of connection with one's self that constitutes the foundation of the overall Gandhian paradigm. Gandhian philosophy of being ethical and moral urges humanity to explore within themselves and look inwards for the knowledge of truth, non-violence and love. Once one is enlightened with truth, it manifests change or transformation, which is referred to as the Gandhian moral paradigm. It can never overlook the 'other' because this realization of morality is never without empathy.

Consequently, the second transformation manifests, changing the relationship with other beings in terms of love, respect and tolerance. This stage of transformation brings about a change in socio-economic and political systems existing among the communities and societies. The significance of cooperation and collective efforts is envisaged, and a non-violent and peaceful social order is established.

The third transformation is that of the relationship of humans with non-human entities. The moral and ethical commitment of the Gandhian paradigm does not cease at human-to-human connections, but is extended to the interconnectedness between human and non-human forms. The ethical and moral responsibility of human existence encourages humans to preserve nature consisting of both transient and permanent elements. To visualize the transformation of the connection between humans and nature or ecology, the spiritual knowledge of truth and non-violence should be present. It is then that the attributes of empathy, love and respect will originate for the entire creation.

Gandhian moral and ethical revolution manifested non-violence and embodied the eternal values of life in his thoughts and actions. He advocated eternal sacredness of life, comprising that of a tree, a plant or even a cow.[77] This was a unique realization: '*vasudevam sarvamidam* (God is all there is)'. He contended, 'The greatness of a nation and its moral progress can be judged by the way its animals are treated.'[78] He always quoted the example of primitive man, who was more compatible with nature and other species and lived in harmony. He believed in the immense power of ahimsa and the littleness of man, and considered humanity a noble attribute of the soul.

The world began to realize the challenge of sustainability—'meeting the needs of the present generation without compromising the ability of future generations to meet their needs'.[79] Later, the notion of sustainable development emerged, enabling human beings to fulfil their aspirations and reach full potential over a sustained period of time.[80] Gradually, the components of SDGs came to be incorporated

---

[77]Gandhi, M.K., *The Voice of Truth*, Shriman Narayan (ed.), Navajivan Publishing House, Ahmedabad, 1968.

[78]Gandhi, M.K., 'Is This Humanity?', *Young India*, Vol. 2, 1924–1926.

[79]'Report of the World Commission on Environment and Development: Our Common Future', United Nations, 1987.

[80]Munasinghe, M., 'Protected Area Economics and Policy: Linking Conservation and Sustainable Development', *Economic and policy Issues in natural Habitats and Protected Areas*, M. Munasinghe and McNeely J. (eds.), World Bank, 1994, pp. 15–49.

in millennium development goals to promote peaceful and inclusive societies for sustainable development, provide access to justice for all, and build effective, accountable and inclusive institutions at all levels.

The evolution of the ESG component in the mid-2000s evidently exhibited the rising consciousness and responsibility of producing sectors in the aspects of environmental challenges and ethical consumption.[81] With growing concern about the ethical status of quoted companies, these standards became the central factors for measuring ethical impact and sustainability of investment in a company. It is crucial to mention that all the elements of SDGs, as well as ESG, were already addressed by the model of Gandhian economics.

Gandhi in *Hind Swaraj* already warned the world of the dangers of environmental destruction, which it faces today.[82] Gandhian thoughts revolutionize the issues of climate change, advocating an environmentally sustainable way of living that sustains an ethical balance between the materialistic needs of humans and their responsibility towards ecology and the environment. He coined the term 'sarvodaya', which reflects 'universal uplift' or 'progress of all'. Gandhi conceived this term, inspired by John Ruskin's notion of political economy—*Unto This Last*.[83] The notion of sarvodaya is based on three basic principles. Firstly, the

[81]Kell, Georg, 'The Remarkable Rise of ESG', *Forbes,* 11 July 2018, https://bit.ly/3ardtiJ. Accessed on 8 July 2022.

[82]Tiwari, Rajnarayan R., 'Gandhi as an Environmentalist', *Indian Journal of Medical Research,* Vol. 149, No. 1, 2019, pp. S141–S143.

[83]Vyas, H.M., (ed.), *Village Swaraj,* Navajivan Publishing House, Ahmedabad, 1963.

good of individuals is contained in the good of all. Secondly, every individual has an equal right to earn a livelihood by working. Finally, the life of labour, such as the life of the tiller of the soil, is worth living.

The concept of sarvodaya stands for 'progress of all', based on equality and liberty. It is an agency of service for common welfare and is based on non-possession, which is a concept of trusteeship. The essence of environmental ethics was advocated through the notion of sarvodaya. Gandhi's vision for the same implied preserving the harmonious existence of humankind with nature and other living beings.[84] Against this backdrop, one of the remarkable movements worth noting is Bhoodan movement. The Bhoodan movement was initiated by Acharya Vinoba Bhave. The movement is also referred to as Bhoodan Pochampally, as it originated in Pochampally in 1951.[85] This movement motivated the wealthy landlords to inculcate a change of heart and imbibe the essence of compassion and a sense of common resource-sharing among the privileged and resourceful. Womenfolk played a critical role in making this movement a success.

The peasants in Andhra Pradesh had called for a violent struggle against the local landlords. However, Bhave, through satyagraha, was able to render a peaceful movement in which the wealthy landlords were motivated to donate a proportion of their landholdings. Vedire Ramachandra Reddy

---

[84]Tiwari, R.R. 'Gandhi as an Environmentalist', *Indian Journal of Medical Research*, Vol. 149, No. 1, p. S141.

[85]Mehta, Subhash, 'Bhoodan-Gramdan Movement-50 Years: A Review', https://bit.ly/3nXyiVT. Accessed on 8 July 2022.

Bhoodan got the title 'Bhoodan' because he was the first donor in Pochampally in Nalgonda district. The movement, later on, developed into Gramdan movement.[86] It further became a part of the sarvodaya society, which entailed the rise of sociopolitical order, recognized for its inclusivity and elements of sustainability, not only across India but the world too. In India, several major movements have been initiated for protecting the environment. Some of the many remarkable movements are Narmada Bachao Andolan, led by Baba Amte and Medha Patkar and the Chipko movement, led by Chandi Prasad Bhatt and Sunderlal Bahuguna. All these movements were highly inspired by Gandhi.

Gandhi identified four main prerequisites for an economically and environmentally sustainable non-exploitative and non-violent economic order.[87] Firstly, there should be a society that condemns greed because greed is the cause of inequality, exploitation, jealousy and conflict. Gandhiji contended that interdependence is inevitable in human society. This interdependence must be based on altruistic values and not on self-interest and materialism. It is only then that *aparigraha* or abstention from acquisitiveness can be practised.[88] This interdependence and cooperation call for immeasurable love for each other. Absolute love should substitute greed. In this respect, the sole aim of cooperation and interdependence of humanity among

---

[86]Ibid.

[87]Joseph, Siby K., *Contextualising Gandhian Thoughts,* Institute of Gandhian Studies, Wardha, 2012, pp. 31–45. https://bit.ly/3RnL0Ld. Accessed on 8 July 2022.

[88]Ibid.

each other and with nature must be to preserve harmony and love.

The next primary notion of Gandhian ideology is that one does not have any right to hold or possess anything that one has not produced. He considered this sort of possession as theft.[89] Therefore, a non-exploitative social order can be visualized on the basis of abstention from all forms of gross and subtle theft, referred to as *asteya*.[90] Thirdly, when one has to abstain from all forms of thefts, one is bound to earn his living based on his labour, and that is referred to as *sharirashram*.[91] Finally, he propagated the notion of 'swadeshi'. This principle of swadeshi originated from the 'law of nature'.[92]

According to Gandhi, all spiritual laws are applicable in day-to-day life. In other words, the true essence of spirituality is embedded in our daily activities. The same is true with the concept of 'swadeshi'—one needs to be self-sufficient. For that, one needs to deploy and utilize all available resources and ensure employment to all in a localized set-up or community. It further implies the protection of one's resources and ensures the availability to all belonging to that region. Harmonizing the availability of local resources among all individuals belonging to a particular locality is the first step towards spiritual connectivity amongst humanity and the spiritual connection humans have with nature.

---

[89]Ibid. 239.

[90]Ibid.

[91]Ibid. 240.

[92]Ibid. 241.

Various ecological scientists and economists have asserted the need for revisiting the harmony between human activities and nature but failed. Harman E. Daly[93] critically analysed the existence of a steady state, while Vivien Stern[94] concluded that economic growth would never result in improvement in environmental quality. A 1995 study concluded that economic growth is not a panacea for environmental quality.[95] Donella Meadows, Jørgen Randers and Dennis Meadows, in their book, *Limits to Growth: The 30-Year Update* (2004) claimed that environmental limits will cause the collapse of the world economic system in the middle of the twenty-first century, given the growth trends in the world population, industrialization, pollution, food production and the rate of depletion of non-renewable resources.[96] It was demonstrated that in the long run, the over-exploitation of resources will become the source of environmental disaster. The projections revealed that there were limits to economic growth owing to the limits on the growth of material throughput for the world economic system.

In 1973, a Norwegian philosopher, Arne Naess coined the term 'deep ecology,' an outlook based on the perception that all living things have value independent of

---

[93]Daly, Herman E., *Steady-State Economics: With New Essays*, Island Press, 1991.

[94]Stern, Vivien, *A Sin against the Future: Imprisonment in the World*, Penguin Books, London, 1998, p. 290.

[95]Arrow, Kenneth, et al., 'Economic Growth, Carrying Capacity, and the Environment', *Ecological Economics*, Vol. 15, No. 2, 1995, pp. 91–5.

[96]Meadows, Donella, et al., *Limits to Growth: The 30-Year Update*, Earthscan, 2005.

their usefulness to other living things. Naess, inspired by Gandhi's notion that all work is important and rather, every work is a form of self-realization, stated that the technique for achieving the power of non-violence is the belief in the essential oneness of all life forms as asserted by Gandhi.[97] This feeling of basic unity overrides all differences and makes them appear superficial. Naess was highly influenced by the Gandhian formulation of non-violence based on the advaitic unity of existence: 'I believe in Advaita, I believe in the essential unity of man and, for that matter, of all that lives. Therefore I believe that if one man gains spiritually, the whole world gains with him and if one man fails, the whole world fails to that extent.'[98] His notion of deep ecology differed from the conventional idea of an environmentalist who values nature as only being useful for human usage.[99] The concept of deep ecology is highly inspired by Gandhian belief in the oneness of all life and, therefore, recognizes the need for conserving resources for the use of all species and not only human beings. Inspired by the notion of Gandhian trusteeship, the argument of deep ecology rejects a world order that only prioritizes the health and well-being of affluent nations.[100]

---

[97]Naess, Arne, 'Gandhi and Group Conflict: An Exploration of Satyagraha, Theoretical Background', *Philosophy East and West*, Vol. 26, No. 1, 1976, pp. 85–8.

[98]Neelakandan, Aravindan, 'The Charkha and the Cow', Swarajya, 25 October 2016, https://bit.ly/3yx2kol. Accessed on 11 July 2022.

[99]Lal, Vinay, 'Gandhi and the Ecological Vision of Life: Thinking Beyond Deep Ecology', *Environmental Ethics*, Vol. 22, No. 2, 2000, pp. 149–68.

[100]Naess, Arne, 'The Deep Ecological Movement: Some Philosophical Aspects', *Philosophical Inquiry*, Vol. 8, No. ½, 1986, pp. 10–31.

Gandhi viewed all spheres of life in an integrated manner.[101] He contended, 'I need no inspiration other than Nature's. She has never failed me as yet. She mystifies me, bewilders me, sends me to ecstasies.' Some of the Gandhian practices were a reflection of spiritual as well as ecological balance. By observing silence, Gandhi was not only communicating with his inner self but also reaching out to the higher energy. This was a remarkable method adopted to conserve one's energy. Such a practice complies with what science refers to as the first law of thermodynamics. He reinforced a connection with ecology by preserving and conserving an ecological balance through his novel idea of fasting, which he practised repeatedly.

The Gandhian idea of the spinning wheel is a phenomenal reflection of the cycle of life. It is not only seen as a technique for meditation, self-realization and self-sufficiency but also represents the biodegradable nature of production. Spinning represents the strength of oneness and mindfulness. It becomes the source of humanity and self-respect. Not deploying machinery in this process and rather using labour is a reflection of conservation of energy and resources.

Gandhi respected all species existing within the surrounding ecosystem. One finds a piece of evidence from his life when he gave clear instructions to not kill a cobra even if it bit him.[102] He wrote, 'I do not want to live at the

---

[101]Tiwari, Rajnarayan R., 'Gandhi as an Environmentalist', *Indian Journal of Medical Research*, Vol. 149, No. 1, 2019, pp. S141–S143.

[102]Lal, Vinay, 'Gandhi and the Ecological Vision of Life', *Environmental Ethics*, Vol. 22, No. 2, 2000, pp. 149–68.

cost of the life even of a snake.'[103] He contended that the lives of all species have descended from the same God. Gandhi considered cow protection as one of the most wonderful phenomena in human evolution.[104] The cow could be viewed as a significant link between humanity and nature, maintaining ecological harmony. The tradition of maintaining vast cattle populations for various economic needs became the source of sustaining the ecological cycle. For India, 'cow', like khadi, is a reflection of the economic symbol of ecological balance, demonstrating a symbiosis between humankind and nature. Moreover, coal- or oil-based economy has not only been environmentally destructive, leading to over-exploitation of limited resources, but has also been the main cause for war, destruction and unrest.

Gandhi was a strong believer in recycling the throughput of humans. He strongly advocated the process of recycling and minimizing waste, and the adoption of a lifestyle that integrates with the ecosystem. According to him, humans must lead a life that converges with the law of nature and maintains ecological harmony. Gandhi believed that having higher intellectual level and wisdom, humans should be more compassionate to lower beings. As a strong supporter of the conservation of natural resources, he appealed to people for recycling and minimizing waste. His ashrams were constructed on wastelands adjacent to villages.[105] He

[103]Gandhi, M.K., *Truth is God,* Navajivan Publishing House, Ahmedabad, 1955, p. 102.

[104]Neelakandan, Aravindan, 'The Charkha and the Cow', Swarajya, 25 October 2016, https://bit.ly/3yx2kol. Accessed on 11 July 2022.

[105]Singh, Savita, *Global Concern with Environmental Crisis and Gandhi's Vision,* S.B. Nangia A.P.H. Publishing Corporation, New Delhi, 1999.

strongly emphasized the importance of keeping one's home and surroundings clean.

Practising silence and fasting were the methods through which Gandhi was attempting to formulate a path or lifestyle that would ensure that the evolution of humankind eventually decreases entropy.

Gandhi's notion of *nayi talim* is a remarkable illustration of imbibing the traditional knowledge of spirituality, academics and life skills in a child. This was a unique method designed by Gandhi to teach every individual, right from his childhood, about the true meaning of connection with ecology and provide training in developing sustainable life skills. These skills originate from the philosophy of 'reduce, reuse and recycle', and provide the source of livelihood for one's lifetime.[106] Gandhi was equally aware and mindful of inculcating good sanitary habits among people and was the biggest advocate for the use of biogas and manure for cooking and other related activities. The model community biogas plants are actively functioning in all the Gandhi ashrams, transforming human waste into organic fertilizers.[107] Several research experiments have examined the efficient usage and recycling of water in toilets.[108]

Gandhi's reverence for life and respect for animals was not confined by intolerance, which he considered another

---

[106]Chanshetti, Umakant, Dr, et al., 'Reduce, Reuse and Recycle: Sense of Responsibility in Mahatma Gandhi Global Village, *International Journal of Current Research*, Vol. 6, No. 9, 2014, pp. 8442–5.

[107]Ibid. 23

[108]Ibid.

name for violence.[109] He was actively tolerant of all humans having diversified food habits, though he was a strict vegetarian.[110] Vinay Lal summarized Gandhi's life in the most appropriate manner: 'Gandhi's entire life functioned much like an ecosystem.'[111] Gandhi's everyday life—every minute act, emotion and thought—was well placed, appropriate and never lacked ethics and morality.

It is, therefore, crucial to revisit the essence of Gandhian thoughts and highlight its underlying message for humanity. Humans need to connect themselves with nature and establish a symbiosis between their needs and ecology. The present socio-economic systems have been unsuccessful in identifying the right lifestyle for humans on earth. In this context, Gandhian ideology illuminates and guides a framework that is not only economically sustainable but also compatible with the environment. In other words, a Gandhian revolution is envisaged in the sphere of economics and issues related to climate change.

It was on Gandhian philosophy that Kumarappa based his economy of permanence. The concept is comparable to 'the cradle-to-cradle' philosophy, which focuses on generating lesser wastage and using renewable sources for production. The concept of 'permanent' is absolute—beyond time and space. The concept can be attributed to God, truth and love, all of which are unchangeable. Within the gambit of time and space, nothing is permanent. For

---

[109]Lal, Vinay, 'Gandhi and the Ecological Vision of Life: Thinking Beyond Deep Ecology', *Environmental Ethics*, Vol. 22, No. 2, 2000, pp. 149–68.
[110]Ibid. 23.
[111]Ibid. 24.

Gandhi, nature was analogous to God. However, when nature is not considered as God, and rather understood as being limited by time and space, then nature will cease to exist sometime in the future. In this context, human life is said to be transient in comparison to nature, which is permanent.[112]

However, it is important to comprehend that nature consists of some materials that are fixed in quantity, such as coal, petroleum, iron, copper etc. These are considered transient.[113] The underlying phenomenon of nature's permanency is based on close cooperation that exists to maintain the continuity of life. Nature has the inherent capacity to support the continuity of life.

This notion of continuity of life is inspired by the Gandhian philosophy of non-violence and absolute love. The moment there is a break in continuity, violence erupts, leading to unrest or conflict. Any kind of violence disrupts harmony and proves to be detrimental to continuity; growth and progress stops, ending in destruction and waste. If humankind pays enough respect to one's work and deeds, and performs daily activities remaining synchronized with the cycle of life; taking into consideration the freedom of fellow humans and other units, it will exist in harmony with the world around and nature. Nature, in return for all the coordination, extends support in the form of air, water and land, thereby, fulfilling the needs of food and nourishment. This doctrine of the cycle of life depicts the fundamentals of the philosophy of 'cradle-

[112]Ibid. 9.
[113]Ibid.

to-cradle' discussed above—what emerges from nature is returned to nature to keep the cycle of life functional.

Gandhi had said, 'There is enough for everybody's needs and not for everybody's greed.' His concept of trusteeship originates from non-possession, emphasizing that possessing material things that we do not need is similar to stealing. The best alternative is to own resources as a custodian of nature. The twin models based on Gandhian philosophy—the trusteeship model and economy of permanence—provide a breakthrough in the perspective of visualizing human's coexistence with nature. The message of honouring nature as the supreme and the most significant entity for human existence has been manifested by the Gandhian revolution for combating climate change. A lifestyle based on self-reliant and non-violent methods or philosophy is critical in visualizing sustainable pathways for climate change.

Gandhi asserted that the noblest way and the purest form in which a human can express love is through his service to fellow human beings. Through this selfless service, he can gain the capability to experience divinity on earth. However, if humankind decides to divert from selfless love to greed and selfishness or shift focus to accumulation of wealth, then this endeavour becomes the cause of all conflicts and proves to be detrimental to the environment and ecological harmony.

Gandhi advocated that when individuals perform their tasks selflessly and are unconditionally inspired to maintain harmony with nature, a non-violent and peaceful society can be visualized. One of the remarkable examples of a cooperative society worth mentioning here is the Milk Cooperative Society, in Nagpur, linked to Goras Bhandar, which originated in 1983.[114] This cooperative society, characterized by transparency, participatory and consensus-based decision-making mechanisms, and a socially inclusive system, became a role model for human values and a peaceful decentralized system.

The more ethical and moral humankind is, the more spiritually evolved it will be. Individual transformation can be brought about only through the moral revolution advocated by Gandhi. Further, only spiritually transformed humankind has the ability to function in cooperation, coordination and collaboration within groups or communities. This synchronized coordination and cooperation can be realized when there is one single cause or aim. Serving humanity by sacrificing self-interests should be the sole purpose. In this respect, Gandhi proposed the trusteeship model, as discussed in Chapter 3, which established the ethical relationship of humans with nature. According to the notion of the trusteeship model, humans serve as custodians of nature and try to restore every part of it or bequeath it to the future generations. This rationality can emerge only when humankind has an ethically evolved consciousness, which is free from self-interest and accumulation.

Morally evolved humankind, which is self-reliant, will be able to distinguish between the ethical minimum

---

[114]Jadhav, Radheshyam, 'Gandhian Principles Help Maharashtra Milk Co-Op Beat the Odds', *Business Line*, 27 September 2020, https://bit.ly/3Pkwylc. Accessed on 11 July 2022.

wants and unlimited desires. Such a society will be free from concentration of power, accumulation of wealth and warfare. Individuals will realize their responsibility towards nature and act as custodians. Wealth will be considered as common for all, and the surplus will be distributed among the weakest and deprived sections. Such a decentralized community will depend on local technology and resources, and will be self-sufficient.

Human existence has proved to be extremely devastating for nature, resulting in over-exploitation and climate change. An enormous stock of ecological footprint has been accumulated over the centuries of human consumption. In other words, the impact of humanity on the environment and the resulting inequalities is evident from the present challenge of climate change. This biggest global challenge is directly linked with the use of conventional energy sources and economic growth.

The conventional sources of energy, most of which are exhaustible sources, such as coal, oil, hydrocarbons, etc., have been in use for centuries. These are responsible for excessive carbon dioxide emissions, which, in turn is responsible for the present climate change. Therefore, energy conservation, transition to renewable sources and efficient usage are the only alternatives to save the planet from the catastrophe of climate change. Identifying energy transition pathways is one of the enormous challenges too. As a consequence, all the nations in the world have moved towards a sustainable development path. In terms of energy, it means shifting to the environmentally sustainable energy sources. In the present global scenario, the concept of SDGs, as discussed, has been framed to incorporate challenges related to energy.[115]

Conventional sources of energy have been the reason behind the concentration of power, violence, warfare and unrest. It has been the main cause behind geopolitical unrest and disorder. Further, human civilization has been marked by subjugation and preponderance of power as a consequence of the act of domination over the limited conventional energy sources, such as oil, natural gas, coal, etc. The conventional energy system has been centralized in most of the countries. Such an energy system usually falls under a locked-in centralization, but has been facing a shift in favour of decentralized initiatives. A decentralized energy system will entail generation of energy sources near the place they will be used, instead of being generated further away from the area, which requires the energy access, and it will be grid-connected. Such an energy framework will be compatible with Gandhian decentralized settings, which are self-sufficient. Within this, the energy requirement will be fulfilled by utilizing localized technology and such communities will be self-sustained and dependent on renewable and clean energy systems.

In the present world, energy is used for transportation, cooking, heating, cooling rooms, manufacturing, etc. Substantial demand for energy consumption depends on how people use it—it could be by turning off machines when not in use or choosing to buy energy-efficient vehicles

---

[115]'Sustainable Development Goal 7', Sustainable Energy for All, https://bit.ly/3nR7lTR. Accessed on 11 July 2022.

and appliances. When it comes to reducing emissions, energy conservation holds a special place. It refers to any behaviour or action that leads to lesser use of energy—like turning off lights while leaving the room, recycling aluminium cans, etc.

Both energy conservation and energy efficiency are concepts concerning the habits of individuals. An evolved consciousness which is sensitive to nature is aware and motivated to preserve harmony with nature. As per the Gandhian ecological revolution, the lesser we consume from the environment, the lesser waste we generate. Such elements are embedded in the genesis of Gandhian thoughts of a non-violent and peaceful economy.

Civilization in the real sense exists not in multiplication but in the deliberate and voluntary reduction of wants.[116] This alone promotes real happiness, contentment and increases the capacity for service. A morally evolved and ethically transformed individual will never ignore the impact of his actions on ecology and environment. In a decentralized set-up, all desires will get replaced by rational needs and human interaction with nature will become confined to a smaller region. Consequently, the energy resources needed to achieve such limited needs will also become minimized. The limited energy requirement will have a direct impact on energy conservation.

In decentralized energy systems, a reduced degree of transmission losses will imply increased conversion

---

[116]*The Collected Works of Mahatma Gandhi, Vol L, June–August 1932*, The Publications Division, Ministry of Information and Broadcasting, Government of India, 1972.

efficiency, increased use of renewable, carbon-neutral and low-carbon fuels, a greater degree of security for businesses and investments. A decentralized energy system will lead to greater flexibility in meeting the local demand patterns for electricity and heat. This will also lead to greater awareness of energy-related issues through community-based energy systems, driving a change in social attitudes, bringing about more efficient use of energy resources.

Several tribal communities in Madhya Pradesh, Bihar, Andhra Pradesh and other states depict an ideal Gandhian community—they make use of simple technology that is not detrimental to the physical, mental and spiritual health of their workers. Such communities represent a self-sufficient energy system. Firewood cut from the community's forest is used for keeping indoors warm, for heating water and cooking. While candles substitute for indoor lightings, cellars function as refrigerators. The community also deploys other indigenous techniques, like water-powered sawmills to generate electricity.

Another example worth mentioning is that of Chhotkei village project in Odisha. The project was undertaken by SunMoksha, which made the village India's first smart-grid village and first smart village.[117] Through consensus-based decisions, this village provides appropriate infrastructure concerning sustainable agriculture, energy sufficiency, rural industries, waste management, health services, education, skill development, e-governance and finally, improved

---

[117]'India's First Smart Village in Chhotkei, Odisha', SunMoksha, https://bit.ly/3o7Nik5. Accessed on 14 July 2022.

connectivity. The basic aim of such an innovative endeavour is to move the communities up the value chain, improving their socio-economic status.[118]

Thus, consensus-based energy systems that use localized energy resources are independent and self-sufficient. Such decentralized community models are the epitome of Gandhian philosophy and signify Gandhian revolution, resolving issues of climate change. Evaluating the emerging concerns raised by ecologists and environmental economists, this chapter demonstrated the relevance of Gandhian transformation and Gandhian economics as the driving force behind ecological sustainability.

Our earth consists of an inexplicable variety of species. Humans constitute a very small proportion of life on this planet—approximately 0.01 per cent.[119] Considering our ecological existence, the significance of life is quite nominal. On the contrary, humankind's impact on ecological balance has been devastating and catastrophic. This is referred to as the ecological footprint of humankind. Gandhi wanted to transform the inner core of humans to relate life and its existence with the context of absolute love. The form of truth or love he envisaged evolved from complete self-sacrifice, transforming the entire purpose of living and existence.

---

[118]Das, Ashok K., Dr, 'Sustainable Energy Access and Security for Rural India', *Energy Security Challenges: Non Traditional Security Planning in India*, CPPR-Centre for Strategic Studies, 2015, https://bit.ly/3yyuO14. Accessed on 11 July 2022.

[119]Ritchie, Hannah, 'Humans Make Up Just 0.01% of Earth's Life–What's the Rest?', Our World in Data, 24 April 2019, https://bit.ly/3ORv3vb. Accessed on 11 July 2022.

A moral revolution can manifest only when humans learn to devote their actions to others selflessly and with love. This will then transform the socio-economic and political relations and how humans interact and perceive nature. It is this moral and ethical revolution that will help humans realize their smallness in front of the vastness of nature.

FIVE

Gandhi: Our Contemporary

It is practically impossible to live in India and not see or hear references of Gandhi. He has, by far, been the most recognizable Indian personality whose image has been printed on currency notes; his statues have been erected in the middle of town squares; his pictures can be seen pasted on the walls of business offices, shops and even restaurants. But, this does not necessarily mean that Gandhi has been well read and understood by all Indians.

A quick look at everyday Indian politics and the debates in the press shows that Gandhi's spirit is no more fully present in his native country. Though his name is taken by all politicians and managers, when it comes to his teachings, young, middle-class technologists, corporate lawyers and businessmen in India consider Gandhi an old-fashioned figure with a preference for an austere and simple lifestyle.

We often ask our students and young Indians about Gandhi's relevance in today's India. 'Gandhi is only a name and an image in India today,' they comment coldly, as if we have been taken in by a romantic view of India, which lived the Gandhian non-violence as a utopian dream, far from the harsh reality of the everyday life of the Indians. Even if there is an ounce of truth in this argument, we need to be reminded that Gandhi has been more appreciated and read seriously outside India than among the last two generations of Indians. Moreover, he remains a towering figure, who seems as fascinating as he was till the time he was assassinated by Nathuram Godse.

The impact of his philosophy of non-violence in inspiring leaders of the twentieth century, such as Khan Abdul Ghaffar Khan, Martin Luther King Jr, Nelson Mandela and Václav Havel, can be invoked as a Gandhian moment. As such, Gandhi's success as a universal dissenter against intolerance and injustice goes far beyond his national stature as the founding father of modern India. Let us not forget that in the past 100 years, his message of non-violent revolt against injustice and fight for human dignity has become a part of the moral conscience of humanity. Undoubtedly, Gandhi inspired the young protesters of Arab Spring and the Iranian Green Movement, both of which lasted from 2009 to 2011. He has also been an inspiration to those who participated in the Black Lives Matter protests following the legacy of Martin Luther King Jr.

Consequently, the Indian youth, in many ways, has been lagging behind the youth of Iran, Hong Kong and Myanmar in practising the Gandhian strategy of non-violence. The reintroduction of Gandhi to the Indian youth by Anna Hazare in 2014 had a short life. The latter's rise was followed by his immediate eclipse in the Indian civil society. Almost eight years down the line, Hazare, who had once a massive Gandhian influence in India, has now become totally irrelevant. The members who earlier supported his anti-corruption movement went on to either join the Bharatiya

Janata Party, formed their own political party (such as the Aam Aadmi Party) or distanced themselves from civic activism. As a matter of fact, in the game of party politics in India and elsewhere, Gandhian principles now stand belittled and ineffective.

Gandhi himself was very well aware of this weakness in his collaboration with the Congress party during the Independence movement. He wrote the following in 1937:

> One interpretation I put upon the India Act is that it is an unconscious challenge to Congressmen to demonstrate the virtue of nonviolence and the sincerity of their conviction about it. If the Congress can give such a demonstration, most of the safeguards fall into desuetude, and the Congress can achieve its goal without a violent struggle, and also without civil disobedience. If the Congress has not impregnated the people with the nonviolent spirit, it has to become a minority, and remain in opposition, unless it will alter its creed.[120]

Had Gandhi been among us today, he would not have collaborated with any of the Indian political parties. Though a political strategist, he was also a moral leader. He himself had said: 'To understand what I say one needs to understand my conduct.'[121] Far from being what he called 'an experiment with truth', politics in contemporary

---

[120]Gandhi, M.K., *Gandhiji Expects*, Navajivan Publishing House, Ahmedabad, 1965, p. 152.

[121]Kolge, Nishikant, *Gandhi Against Caste*, Oxford University Press, New Delhi, 2017, p. 1.

India is about winning elections. Indian politics has never been so un-Gandhian—it now seems to be a prisoner of the administrative system and the corporate mindset, both of which suffer from a severe lack of self-examination. In a sense, Gandhi would have been troubled by the Machiavellian essence of Indian politics, and its populist and demagogic end results. This does not necessarily mean that Gandhi was a pure idealist. Actually, he was a pragmatic practitioner, who wanted to apply ethical values and civilizational criteria to the political organization of Indian society and beyond. Yet, strangely enough, the Gandhian common sense is considered an irrelevant and insignificant matter to the eyes of those who are ruling India and the world today. Unfortunately, in today's world, political circumstances and temperaments do not allow politicians to concentrate any more on the education and duty of citizens. That is why, while uncritical and utilitarian minds are shaped and formed in universities across India and around the world, the originality and exemplarity of future personalities, like him, are killed at the embryonic stage.

Very few people engaged in Indian politics understand Gandhi's moral suffering with the Machiavellian mindset. With the exception of Khan Abdul Ghaffar Khan, who earned the moniker 'Frontier Gandhi', the closest collaborators of Gandhi in the Congress party were worried with what they considered as 'Gandhi's quixotism'. However, during his 30 years of political life in India, Gandhi was incessantly aware of the fact that the Congress would turn a deaf ear to his ideas expressed in the *Hind Swaraj*. Nearly four-and-a-half months before Independence, he confessed:

> I do not matter in the scheme of things today. If I did, [the insanity in] Punjab would not have happened, nor Bihar, nor Noakhali. No one listens to me today. I am a very small man. Yes, I was once a big man in Hindustan. Everybody listened to me. Today the Congress does not heed me, nor do the Hindus, nor the Muslims... Mine is a cry in the wilderness.[122]

In a sense, in post-Independence India, power politics and populism wiped away the Gandhian legacy of spiritual politics. Truly, Gandhi's critique of religious fanaticism was one of the greatest Socratic gestures of his intellectual self-examination. Such an attitude of mind was represented by Gandhi's intuitive approach to truth, which was the foundation of his epistemic humility and his interfaith dialogue. A striking feature of Gandhi's civic spiritualism was his insistence that India is not an exclusively Hindu civilization. His political genius lay in reconciling the complex social and religious fabric of traditional Indian society with the modern phenomenon of swaraj and the struggle for independence. As such, more than being the 'father of the nation', he could be remembered as the architect of an interfaith and intercultural India. Gandhi gave different religious communities, for the first time, a sense of involvement in the country's destiny. Though he made civic spirituality an integral part of swaraj, he abstained from any reference to Hinduism, Islam, Buddhism or Jainism in his definition of self-governance and self-realization.

---

[122]Chandra, Sudhir, *Gandhi: An Impossible Possibility*, Chitra Padmanabhan (trans.), Routledge, 2017, p. 9.

He continually defined and defended Indian nationalism through his belief in the truth of all religions.

Until the end of his life, Gandhi was very clear about his attitude toward Hinduism. What distinguished him from most of his Hindu and Muslim friends and collaborators was that for him, the question of religion was more ethical and spiritual than political. As mentioned previously, he refused to see religion with a fanatic perspective. He, therefore, left the religion of temples, mosques and churches, and replaced it with his quest for truth. The goal of that spiritual exercise was to purify hearts and remove arrogance, bitterness and violence. No matter how difficult the task, Gandhi realized that in his encounter with the 'moral degeneration' [words used by him] of the Congress party, he was all alone in trying to transcend and to correct the evils of the religions. Gandhi's letter to Jawaharlal Nehru on 2 May 1933 is a perfect example of his difficult journey with religious fanaticism, despite his love for Hinduism. He wrote:

> The Harijan movement is too big for mere intellectual effort. There is nothing so bad in all the world. And yet I cannot leave religion and therefore Hinduism. My life would be a burden to me if Hinduism failed me. I love Christianity, Islam and many other faiths through Hinduism. Take it away from me and nothing remains for me. But then I cannot tolerate it with untouchability—the high-and-low belief. Fortunately Hinduism contains a sovereign remedy for the evil. I have applied the remedy... And surely death is not an end to all effort. Rightly faced, it may be but the

> beginning of a nobler effort. But I won't convince you by argument, if you did not see the truth intuitively.[123]

A serious reader of Gandhi would know the extent to which he was committed to non-orthodox Hinduism, the roots of which he found in the Bhagavad Gita. What interested Gandhi in the Gita was the notion of selfless and detached action, which results from a devotion to truth. In the Gita, he also found a philosophical foundation for his politics of inclusion. As he affirmed:

> Almost every page of the Gita advises us not to make a distinction between our people and others. How is this to be done? Reflection will lead us to the conclusion that we should perform all our acts in a spirit of non-attachment... In every chapter the Gita brings out how such a distinction is false and harmful.[124]

It is clear that Gandhi choosing the Gita was a way for him to define Hinduism in terms of sacrifice and service and rejection of all forms of egocentrism. Peace and non-violence, as Gandhi understood it, would not be achieved through any one single religion but would be the outcome of a dialogue among all faiths. Gandhi's views on Hindu–Muslim unity, untouchability and the caste system were outputs of his pluralistic vision of religion and faith. As such, it is practically impossible to make a fundamentalist out of Gandhi. He was not a temple-goer and none of his ashrams

---

[123]Ibid. 138–9.

[124]Iyer, Raghavan (ed.), *The Essential Writings of Mahatma Gandhi*, Oxford University Press, New Delhi, 1990, p. 70.

were built on the philosophical fundamentals of the caste system. And above all, he asserted:

> I exercise my judgment about every scripture, including the Gita. I cannot let a scriptural text supersede my reason. Whilst I believe that the principal books are inspired, they suffer from a process of double distillation. Firstly, they come through a human prophet, and then through the commentaries of interpreters. Nothing in them comes from God directly.[125]

During the last years of his life, Gandhi was plainly advocating the end of caste differences and prejudices in Hindu society. From his point of view, such a change and transformation were only possible through his vision of swaraj. In his famous letter to Nehru, he wrote:

> I still stand by the system of Government envisaged in Hind Swaraj. These are not mere words. All the experience gained by me since 1908 [sic] I wrote the booklet has confirmed the truth of my belief. Therefore, if I am left alone in it I shall not mind, for I can only bear witness to the truth as I see it.[126]

Undoubtedly, Gandhi's ideas were within the reach of Indian society, but India did not choose the path of Gandhi. However, his philosophy is still very relevant to Indians and to others, and significant to contemporary global challenges.

---

[125]*Collected Works of Mahatma Gandhi, Vol. LXIV, November 3, 1936–March 14, 1937,* The Publications Division, Ministry of Information and Broadcasting, Government of India, 1976, p. 75.

[126]Kolge, Nishikant, *Gandhi Against Caste*, Oxford University Press, New Delhi, 2017, p. 197.

With this in mind, it can be said that Gandhi was oriented towards reinventing politics as tools for self-realization and self-transformation of society. Maybe this is why each time we read a page on Gandhi, we are tempted to go back to the youth around the world and ask them to revisit him as an invaluable thinker and moral guide amid the political problems and the cultural confusions in which we live.

A legal system or a regime is critical to the foundation of a resilient society. Any governance, state or region that has a strong and comprehensive legal base will foster and deliver justice, equity and inclusivity, all of which are accessible and affordable to every individual. Gandhi's exemplary inclination towards truth made him the extraordinary human who raised his voice against injustice and subjugation. The judicial system, from the Gandhian perspective, originated from the basic and elementary notion of justice prevailing at an institution existing at the ground level. Justice at the grassroots level was delivered through panchayat system.

> Village panchayats as the self-sustainable democratic unit were placed at the center of the constitutional framework. A village panchayat is largely a self-sustainable democratic method of governance and functioning, aiming toward a decentralized model of governance. The Gandhian vision of the constitution was a quest for swaraj, a manifesto against government regulation, demand for freedom, and his civilizational ideal of Ramaraj.[127]

---

[127] Shrivastava, Anujaya, et al., 'Mahatma Gandhi and law: A historico-legal perspective', *The Daily Guardian*, 2 October 2021, https://bit.ly/3PjOpsQ. Accessed on 11 July 2022.

'In my heart of hearts, I always wished that I should win only if my client's case was right.'[128] As the custodian of ethical responsibility, he never accepted a false case and considered it his utmost duty to not deceive the court. He never lost faith in law, but lost faith in the traditional legal system, such as courts, judges, lawyers and litigation.[129] 'It was not impossible to practice law without compromising the truth. Even truthfulness in the practice of the profession cannot cure it of the fundamental defect that vitiates it.'[130] He had immense respect for law and he even respected the laws of the British parliament. It is evident from all the activities organized as part of satyagraha across the country. The civil disobedience movement, called by Gandhi, presented a great difficulty for the British, as satyagrahis never resisted arrest or punishment. All protests were peaceful demonstrations.[131]

Further, Gandhi believed that the Indian justice system rewarded the wealthy and compounded the miseries of the poor, yet he contended that lawyers should place 'truth and service' above the perks of the profession.[132] O.P. Motiwal

---

[128]Gandhi, M.K., *An Autobiography: The Story of My Experiments with Truth*, Beacon Press, 1993, pp. 361–2.

[129]Shrivastava, Anujaya, et al., 'Mahatma Gandhi and Law: A Historico-Legal Perspective', *The Daily Guardian*, 2 October 2021, https://bit.ly/3PjOpsQ. Accessed on 11 July 2022.

[130]Gandhi, M.K., *The Story of My Experiments with Truth*, Navajivan Publishing House, 1959, p. 269.

[131]Satyaranjan C. Dharmadhikari, Justice, 'In Order to "Indianise" Justice Delivery Systems, We Must Follow the Gandhian Way', *The Leaflet*, 2 October 2021, https://bit.ly/3c5uzTy. Accessed on 11 July 2022.

[132]Shrivastava, Anujaya, et al., 'Mahatma Gandhi and Law: A Historico-Legal Perspective', *The Daily Guardian*, 2 October 2021, https://bit.ly/3PjOpsQ. Accessed on 11 July 2022.

stated that Gandhi once remarked 'Facts mean truth, and once we [lawyers] adhere to truth, the law comes to our aid naturally,' while he reflected his experiences as a lawyer in South Africa.[133]

Highlighting the benefits of out-of-court settlements, from the experiences in South Africa, Gandhi stated, 'I had learned the true practice of law. I had learnt to find out the better side of human nature and to enter men's hearts. I realized that the true function of a lawyer was to unite parties driven as under.'[134] In the context of the role of legislation in eradicating social injustice, Gandhi believed, 'There is no doubt that untouchability is a mental attitude. It cannot be abolished by legislation. Law can touch the body, but not the mind. The mind can be touched only by love and persuasion.'[135]

'Justice should become cheap and expeditious. Today it is the luxury of the rich and the joy of the gambler.'[136] While emphasizing on the role of democracy in ensuring justice, Gandhi contended, 'It was the function of democracy to make justice cheap and expeditious and to ensure all possible purity in the administration... No minister has the right to interfere with the course of justice, even for his dearest ones.'[137]

---

[133]Ibid.

[134]Ibid.

[135]*The Collected Works of Mahatma Gandhi, Vol. LIV, October 13, 1931–February 8, 1932,* The Publications Division, Ministry of Information and Broadcasting, Government of India, 1973, p. 325.

[136]Gupta, Prashant, *Wisdom of Gandhi*, Ocean Books, New Delhi, 2009, p. 96.

[137]Tendulkar, D.G., *Mahatma: Life of Mohandas Karamchand Gandhi-Vol. 8,* The Publications Division, Ministry of Information and Broadcasting, Government of India, 1954, p. 193

The respect, conviction and faith for the nation's legal system and institution held by the State, individual and bureaucracy are of enormous significance. All conflict resolution and discontent in socio-economic and political spheres can be unfolded with a strong foundation of the legal framework. Gandhi asserted that it is imperative for democratic governance that we have our own justice delivery system. He contended that laws should be formulated in a consensus-based, democratic way and then implemented through a well-established and profound legal regime. Public policy functions efficiently and effectively only with the systematic support of a robust legal structure. Gandhi advocated for our own distinct jurisprudence and legal principles of statutory interpretation.[138] However, we lost him too early before his ideas of a justice delivery system could be implemented. According to Gandhi, the British judicial officers never imparted justice to all. The justice delivery system under the British was expensive and not affordable to all sections of society. It was a privilege benefitting only the rich and powerful.

A peaceful and non-violent society envisages the preservation of rights of every individual and is one wherein maintenance of rights is regulated lawfully. Finally, the vision of India in the Preamble to our Constitution envisions equality, justice and fair treatment for all, irrespective of one's social or economic status.[139] However, this is impossible

---

[138]C. Dharmadhikari, Satyaranjan, Justice, 'In Order to "Indianise" Justice Delivery Systems, We Must Follow the Gandhian Way', *The Leaflet*, 2 October 2021, https://bit.ly/3c5uzTy. Accessed on 11 July 2022.
[139]Ibid.

without the uniform application of laws. The role of a profound and robust legal framework is necessary not only at the regional and local level but also at the international level to safeguard the rights of individuals or stakeholders whose freedoms bear the risk of being compromised in any sense. The Gandhian perspective of formulating international law or even the regional legal framework must be more democratic, involving the consent of every individual. It is only then that a non-violent and peaceful state, region or country can be visualized. In addition, a decentralized system, based on a democratic decision-making process, a robust legal and regulatory regime, will establish a peaceful and sustainable society.

There have been systematic attempts by several economists, ecologists and environmentalists to resolve the emerging global challenges. The discipline of economics revolves around the basic economic problem of scarcity because human wants are unlimited, while resources are not. The failure of economic growth models to attain inclusive growth, poverty alleviation and reduction in inequality make it imperative to revisit the prevailing models of growth and development. In India, about 400 million workers in the informal economy were at the highest risk of descending further into poverty during the crisis of Covid-19 pandemic.[140]

It is evident that in all the development debates till now, regional inequality had been ignored. It is also evident that elements and aspects of Gandhian economics have now

---

[140]'LO Monitor: COVID-19 and the World of Work. Second Edition Updated Estimates and Analysis', International Labour Organization, 7 April 2020, https://bit.ly/3c1w990. Accessed on 14 July 2022.

started finding their presence in some way or the other in economics as a discipline, as the latter has attempted to rectify its fundamentals to incorporate broader issues, such as inequality, climate change and environmental degradation.

Welfare economics, which is another branch of the discipline, attempted to measure the well-being of the worst-off individuals. Thus, a utilitarian approach evolved to visualize a general equilibrium. However, welfare economics failed to address the challenges related to the environment and ecology. From the utilitarian perspective, the Rawlsian welfare approach attempted to resolve the question of justice and equitable distribution, proposing a similar notion as advocated by Gandhi.

The notion of a cradle-to-cradle sustainable system, which originated in 2001, is a cyclical system where all the materials and products need to be kept clean (such that they do not add to carbon emissions) and should not be mixed. All the resources are used effectively and in a cyclical way. It is contrary to the cradle-to-grave system, which is linear. The concept of cradle-to-cradle system is comparable to Kumarappa's notion of economy of permanence, based on the Gandhian thoughts of reducing wastage and using renewable sources in production processes. Much before the climate change debate began, Gandhi had said that we should act as 'trustees' and use natural resources wisely as it is our moral responsibility to ensure that we bequeath to the future generations a healthy planet.

Mainly evolved in western societies, with its dimensions advancing over time, the concept of corporate social responsibility (CSR) has economic, social and environmental dimensions. It promotes and incorporates sustainable and inclusive investment process. Earlier, social welfare was ensured only at a limited scale in the form of the construction of hospitals and provision of food coupons. CSR originated as an obligation of businessmen to pursue welfare policies with the motive and intention of working towards a society that had higher ethical values. A certain socially responsible business decision can be justified on the grounds of its long-run economic gains and its socially responsible nature. Further, CSR encourages corporate managers to be considered as public trustees through the shareholding system. Thus, the elements of Gandhian thoughts are very much embedded in this notion of CSR, which attempts to incorporate social and ethical responsibility through all agents in society.

However, in the case of emerging global value chains, CSR is a next-to-impossible proposition. CSR, therefore, becomes more challenging than governance, assessment and information management. The notion of CSR brings forth increased spending on sectors, such as education, healthcare and rural development. In addition to CSR, SDGs provided a wider spectrum of targets for ending poverty, reducing inequality, building resilient infrastructure and promoting sustainable use of the terrestrial ecosystem. Gradually, the components of SDGs have been incorporated into millennium development goals, with the aim of promoting peaceful and inclusive societies for sustainable development, providing access to justice for all, and building effective, accountable and inclusive institutions at all levels.

Both the models based on Gandhian ideology are the most robust and resilient, and have survived the attributes of time and space. They offer not only the most sustainable explanations for all contemporary challenges but also withstand the austerity of circumstances. They adapt and evolve efficiently in any era, any society and any nation. They will encourage humans to have ethical and moral thoughts. It is this ethical revolution that ensures socio-economic and environmental sustainability.

Consequently, Gandhi was trying to make the most of the notions of individual autonomy and self-reliant village, both of which he considered to be the two main pillars of the political and economic society of independent India. As such, his picture of a self-realized and decentralized Indian society was totally different from the State-oriented India that Nehru had in his mind. Unlike Nehru, Gandhi knew well that a civil society dominated India and not a British-style parliament, and techno-scientific progress would preserve the social and political cooperation and interconnectedness among the Indians. He wrote:

> We have long been accustomed to think that power comes only through Legislative Assemblies. I have regarded this belief as a grave error brought about by inertia or hypnotism. A superficial study of British history has made us think that all power percolates to the people from parliaments. The truth is that power resides in the people and it is entrusted for the time being to those whom they may choose as their representatives. Parliaments have no power or even existence independently of the people. It has been my effort for the last twenty-one years to convince the people of this simple truth. Civil disobedience is the

> storehouse of power. Imagine a whole people unwilling to conform to the laws of the legislature, and prepared to suffer the consequences of non-compliance! They will bring the whole legislative and executive machinery to a standstill. The police and the military are of use to coerce minorities however powerful they may be. But no police or military coercion can bend the resolute will of a people who are out for suffering to the uttermost. And parliamentary procedure is good only when its members are willing to conform to the will of the majority. In other words, it is fairly effective only among compatibles.
>
> Here in India, we have been pretending to work the parliamentary system under separate electorates which has created artificial incompatibles. Living unity can never come out of these artificial entities being brought together on a common platform.[141]

History shows that Gandhi was right. But India chose Nehru's vision of society, politics and economy. Gandhi's idea of the constructive programme survived, yet, it was applied on a small scale.

Mahatma Gandhi was assassinated by the power of fanaticism before the Indian constitution was framed and finalized. The irony is that members of the Constituent Assembly had Gandhi in their hearts, but not in their minds. As a result, little attention was given to the autonomy of

---

[141] *Collected Works of Mahatma Gandhi, Vol. LXXV, October 11, 1941–March 31, 1942,* The Publications Division, Ministry of Information and Broadcasting, Government of India, 1979, p. 148.

rural India and to the concept of decentralization of political power. The independence of India arrived in the form of a constitutional state and not the swaraj that Gandhi had in mind. However, for Indians and for people around the world, the fact remains: if India is a democracy today, it is due to the efforts of Mahatma Gandhi.

SIX

Thinking with Gandhi

Gandhi's influence on the course of contemporary India and the world in the past 100 years has been immense and significant. In his highly distinctive way, he introduced us to a radical mode of thinking and a simpler way of living.

Author Aditya Nigam said:

> It is worth bearing in mind that when he wrote *Hind Swaraj*, Gandhi, far removed for the world of politics in India, had already set the stage for this lifelong drama. Reading John Ruskin's *Unto This Last* on an overnight train journey, his imagination had been so fired that he had decided to "change my life in accordance with the ideals of that book." The Phoenix Settlement that emerged as a result, in 1904, was an agricultural settlement, which was to be followed in 1910 by the Tolstoy Farm on a much larger area of land. These farms or settlements were meant to instantiate and preserve a way of life that Gandhi, like his soul-mates Ruskin and Tolstoy, saw to be under threat from modern civilisation... The Phoenix Settlement and Tolstoy Farm were acts of the larger drama where Gandhi, determined to refuse modern

> industrial civilisation the satisfaction of consigning entire ways of life to the domain of 'the past', would ceaselessly struggle to find an aesthetic of slowness and simplicity.[142]

The importance that Gandhi gave to simple living, what might be called his existential imperative, can be traced in his moral and political philosophies. He possessed the nobility of spirit and the excellence that could underpin ethics and morality in everyday life. As such, his epistemic strategy was a Socratic one, which led him to a critical examination of his life and reality in general. This change of conduct to a meditative state of thinking, rather than a calculative and instrumentalist one, was not guaranteed by a linear rationality or a pre-established body of ethical knowledge. Actually, what lead Gandhi to a simple life and to the possibility of living it with others was a personal commitment to what he called his 'inner voice'. Socrates talked about his inner voice as a daimonion, an inexplicable divine sign. However, Gandhi never admitted explicitly that his inner voice was the voice of God. For him, it was rather a voice of conscience, distinguished from that of reason. He observed:

> It is true that I do not depend upon my intellect to decide upon any action. For me the reasoned course of action is held in check subject to the sanction of the inner voice. I do not know if others would call

---

[142]Nigam, Aditya, 'Gandhi–The "Angel of History": Reading Hind Swaraj Today', *Economic and Political Weekly*, Vol. 44, No. 11, 2009, p. 44.

> it the mysterious power or whatsoever. I have never deliberated upon this nor analysed it, I have felt no need of doing so either. I have faith, and knowledge, too, that a Power exists beyond reasoning.[143]

For Gandhi, the inner voice essentially showed the limits of rational knowledge in communicating an existential and moral experience. But, the questioning itself, as a spiritual activity, was considered by Gandhi as an ethical act. This is mainly because the Gandhian philosophy is not the solitary construction of a system of thought, but an awakening of consciousness and an accession to a level of plurality that can only be realized by relating with the otherness of the other.

Thus, if we consider the entire Gandhian philosophy as a spiritual exercise and a way of life, we can clearly understand the moral and political significance of the Gandhian reversal of epistemic values and the change he seeks in the guiding principles of life. In other words, Gandhi's merit, in our view, is that he thought about the fundamental unit of existence, that is, the individual, and its responsibilities towards life in general. This leaves us with a Gandhian concern regarding ontology in favour of the ethical. Gandhi placed the concept of responsibility in the relationship between the political and the spiritual. As such, he did not consider freedom a mere pursuit of selfish aims at the expense of others. His insistence on self-realization, as an examination of oneself, demanded that each individual search for freedom not as

---

[143]Gandhi, Gopalkrishna (ed.), *The Oxford India Gandhi: Essential Writings*, Oxford University Press of India, New Delhi, 2008, p. 38.

an individual quest, but as a civic task of self-governance. Thus, Gandhi said that social responsibility and a sense of human interconnectedness go hand in hand. In other words, he believed that all living beings, and not only humans, are part of one another and violence destructs this universal inclusivity. This is the 'cosmic companionship',—as Martin Luther King Jr would call it—that would overcome evils of arrogance, pride and greed.

As indicated all throughout this book, the uniqueness and originality of the Gandhian revolution rested in its conscious efforts to not only overcome the political challenges of India but also to confront the universal and fundamental question of violence. As Nigam put it interestingly, 'The Gandhian intervention was not merely an intervention in the specifics of the Indian political conjuncture at different critical moments; it was an intervention through which a certain "elemental experience" of epic proportions spoke out.'[144] As a matter of fact, Gandhi was not thinking in the direction of the utilitarian philosophy, that ethics should aim at greater happiness for a greater number of people. He defined modernity by its existential essence, rather than by its instrumental goals. Thus, we can say that since the publication of his seminal pamphlet, *Hind Swaraj* in 1909, Gandhi had a bigger picture in mind in his critique of modernity. What Gandhi criticized beyond the instrumental dimensions of railways and factories, is the essence of technology itself, which is the expression of despiritualization of modern life.

---

[144]Nigam, Aditya, 'Gandhi–The "Angel of History": Reading Hind Swaraj Today', *Economic and Political Weekly*, Vol. 44, No. 11, 2009, p. 46.

As a result, Gandhi's impact on modern thought arose from his insistence that what we know is of a lesser value than what we do with our knowledge. As such, the essence of the Gandhian revolution is to confront a series of illusionary comforts that modern technology and modern politics pretend to provide for human beings. Consequently, Gandhi's spiritual existentialism was based on a trust in the goodness of human nature and a belief in a spiritual foundation for ethics that relies on a continuous self-examination. In such existential and experiential journey, modern politics and modern technology can clearly obscure the individual need to find one's own way with truth.

For Gandhi, as for Socrates, virtue was excellence, and the source of this excellence lay with the individual's commitment to an examination of their life. Or to put it like Socrates, 'The unexamined life is not worth living.'[145] In an important sense, to understand the Gandhian revolution in the fields of politics, ethics and economics, one needs to dare to hold their own experiment with truth by creating a code for respecting life. Under such circumstance, conventional politics and ethics, far from being useful signposts in one's existential journey, become true obstacles in the way through which individuals may gain control over themselves.

As it was observed previously, Gandhi argued that real self-rule (swaraj) is as much the acquisition of 'inward freedom' as 'outward freedom' in terms of self-government. Gandhi had said, 'Control over the mind is alone necessary

[145]Plato, *Complete Works*, John M. Cooper and D.S. Hutchinson (eds.), Hackett Publishing, Indianapolis, 1997, p. 33.

and when it is attained, man is free.'[146] Therefore, we can say that in Gandhi's eyes, spiritual self-realization and political self-government are linked as the twin daughters of the same mother—swaraj. Swaraj, therefore, becomes an imperative tool in tackling any human challenge, be it spiritual, ethical, political or environmental. That is to say, Gandhi never believed in shortcuts to success. If Gandhi was the right leader at the right moment in Indian history, it is not because he was a dreamer, but because he had the ability to put an end to the age-old tension between ethics and politics. Gandhi's spiritual humanism was a message of both ethical and political commitments—to take responsibility for social injustice in India, and also for the violence that was happening around the world. He, thereby, laid the foundation for a revolution of values in India and beyond, far above the ideals and actions of any other Indian of his generation. This certainly had to do with his courage to seek truth and his ability to reform himself. He knew well that every human being possesses, at the same time, the capacity of love and the element of bestiality.

Economic and social theorist, Jacques Attali, said, 'While all the other revolutionary leaders were content to draw up plans to change the world from their offices, he did not want to impose a "new man", he was going to become one himself, and then convince others by his sacrifice. He would rather set an example than lecture others.'[147] It is,

[146]Gandhi, Mahatma, *The Collected Works of Mahatma Gandhi, Vol. X, November 1909–March 1911*, The Publications Division, Ministry of Information and Broadcasting, Government of India, pp. 50–1.

[147]Attali, Jacques, *Gandhi ou l'éveil des humiliés*, Fayard, 2007, p. 506.

thus, no exaggeration to say that Gandhi continues to remain an exemplar of total moral and spiritual integrity. The reason for this rests in how he lived and what he did, rather than when and why he died a martyr.

The Gandhian paradigm is nowhere more apparent than in his wholehearted rejection of the Procrustean views of moral and political progress in modern times, which has a disastrous impact on the economic agency and ecological vision of humanity. His political revolution was a total negation of the realist political theory grounded in the Hobbesian assumption that human beings are naturally avaricious. Assessing the nature of political relationship among the actors instead of between the political parties or the states, Gandhi directly challenged the normative legitimacy of modern politics by placing political struggle in the domain of public opinion. His insistence on individual responsibilities and self-governed social movements created a new opportunity for the exercise of pluralistic and empathetic citizenship.

Today, with the emergence of global civil society, we can see up to what point the Gandhian political revolution succeeded in suggesting different sets of priorities than those traditionally associated with the state system. It goes without saying that the Gandhian paradigm contributes directly to the creation of present and future modes of global governance, deriving not exclusively from State-centered hierarchies, but from decentralized discourse and action of citizens around the world. Furthermore, in re-evaluating and rejecting the realist paradigm, the Gandhian paradigm replaced violence with non-violence as a prevalent component of local politics and global relations. As such, by transcending and transforming the realist thought, he annulled the idea of violence as a central concept to relations among states, thus, superseding Carl Philipp Gottfried von Clausewitz's classic definition of war as a mere continuation of policy by other means. It is clear, then, that the Gandhian paradigm of politics remains essentially post-Hobbesian and post-Clausewitzian.

There are two points that should be highlighted here. First, the Gandhian paradigm goes beyond India, so it doesn't belong to Indians alone. Therefore, Gandhi stands in the history of modernity as a critic of all forms of political and normative philosophies which have been in search of uniformity and homogenization. The challenge, for Gandhi, was to focus on the process of building a democratic consciousness, which could provide continuity to the political structures of democracy by way of contrast with all forms of authoritarian and hierarchical traditions. Secondly, there can certainly be no 'democratization' of our democracies or escape from authoritarian and populist regimes in our world without a strong strategy of non-violent disobedience and creative dissent. Gandhi knew that one cannot be a friend of truth without keeping oneself alert in order to be able to distinguish between a false sense of belonging and respect for a common space, where the plurality of voices can be realized.

In a Socratic manner, Gandhi had an acute sense of listening to his inner voice. He referred to his inner voice as a truth force that would lead him to peaceful solutions in life. As a matter of fact, his commitment to speaking truth was parallel, in many respects, to Socrates' reliance on outspokenness (parrhesia). Had he been amongst us today, he would have certainly suggested that we learn to develop our capacity for disobedience and dissent. In many ways, he would not have approved the mediocre and corrupted level of party politics in today's liberal democracies. For him, insistence on ethical renewal of democracy went hand in hand with character-building (moral leadership) and enlightened citizenship (democratic passion).

Unfortunately, the unbearable mediocrity of our era will doubtlessly reduce the nobility of spirit of disobedient and subversive thinkers and practitioners like Gandhi to oblivion. To tell the truth, Gandhian thoughts have never declined so much as when they involve no risks and no dangers. Indians and others cannot read, understand and practise his thoughts without taking risks in their lives. So today, at last, when we have to face real dangers, like climate change, pandemics and mobocracy in our social and political life, there is a chance that Gandhi may be looked upon again.

The basis of the Gandhian revolution—inner voice and interconnectedness—will be the guiding force for every generation. The future generations will recognize the virtue of the Gandhian paradigm not only in India but across the globe. They will relive and keep on reinventing Gandhi in every era simply because humanity has no other option than to come closer and closer to reality and the truth. Wherever truth is the matter of concern, the Gandhian revolution becomes the torchbearer. His pursuit for truth and non-violence can be realized at multiple levels of human life. The transformation of 'inner self', the driving force, also referred to as 'soul force', continues to transform the system of socio-economic and political framework synthesized by evolved humankind.

The interconnectedness of the soul force with the otherness of others can be described as the awakening of consciousness that manifests the Gandhian revolution in every sphere and aspect of life—socio-economic, political and ecological. The Gandhian economic revolution constitutes moral and ethical responsibility to uplift and enrich human life. The component of rationality, which is embedded in the modern economic phenomenon, was revolutionized by Gandhi to visualize economics beyond the scope of optimizing material gains.

To achieve at least the minimal possible respect for human and social values is the key objective of Gandhian economics. Thus, it seeks to attain the ultimate satisfaction. Economics of today's world leads to greed, competition, vested interest and preponderance of power, while equity and distribution are conveniently ignored. Thus, concentrated power in the hands of a few and excessive consumerism have become the fundamentals of today's economics. It gives no quarter to capitalism, but gives the present owning class a chance at reforming itself. It is based on the faith that human nature is never beyond redemption.[148]

Gandhian economics is fundamentally distinct from the classical school of thought, where the 'invisible hands' provide the optimal equilibrium. In Gandhian economics, the inner voice or soul force is the guiding mechanism

---

[148]Gandhi, M.K., *Trusteeship*, Kelkar Ravindra (ed.), Navajivan Mudranalaya, Ahmedabad, 1955, pp. 3–4.

to attain the well-being of humankind. The conventional notion of market mechanism has led to unprecedented consumerism and capitalism, resulting in an unequal world full of unrest and disorder. Later, neo-classical economic thought advocated the role of the State to visualize optimal equilibrium. However, the State failed to serve humanity owing to the fundamental fault in their interest or objective.

The State was guided by vested interests, and political economy played a substantial role in the distribution of wealth and benefits. The primary motive of the State was adulterated by the concentration of power, which further led to domination and warfare. '[...] in the context of the failure of most of the dominant ideologies of the twentieth century, including Marxism and liberalism in its variant forms, there is a strong tendency among the sensitive minds from all over the world to look at Gandhian ideas as providing a new paradigm for an alternative civilisational framework.'[149] Thus, his remarkable work, *Hind Swaraj*, became the source of the new intellectual quest.[150] Gandhi anticipated some disastrous consequences of modern civilization.[151] The detrimental consequences included ecological imbalances, problems of climate change, concentration of power in hands of a few and marginalization of millions.

Neither the markets nor the State have been able to

[149]Pradhan, Ram Chandra, 'Gandhi's Hind Swaraj: A Summary and Centennial View', Bombay Sarvodaya Mandal & Gandhi Research Foundation, https://bit.ly/3NYmNsa. Accessed on 12 July 2022.

[150]Ibid.

[151]Gandhi, M.K., *'Hind Swaraj' and Other Writings*, Anthony J. Parel (ed.), Cambridge University Press, Cambridge, 1997.

deliver an equitable and just society that is inclusive and where each individual acts according to their evolved consciousness, which is not only responsible for every action but also interconnected with other humans and the ecosystem. Such universal upliftment and progress of all was exemplified by the concept of sarvodaya, coined by Gandhi. This, he said, was one of the pillars to support hind swaraj.[152] This concept became the source of service for the common welfare, emphasizing primarily on moral and spiritual values. The philosophy entailed that the rich and the poor give up their materialistic belongings and strive to work for the good of all. Various leaders and civil society workers in India undertook this concept for the purpose of the larger good of society. Some of them worth mentioning are Vinoba Bhave, J.P. Narayan, Dada Dharmadhikari, Dhirendra Mazumdaar, etc.[153]

Gandhian economics has enough space for the State, but the kind of State that was visualized by Gandhi was the one that served humanity. According to Gandhian thoughts, the purpose of economic development is defeated when the system of governance is not aligned to serve humanity in the true sense. Human development devoid of human service is harmful and destructive. His notion of State was a decentralized system of governance based on the decision-making process that worked on consensus. It was about a system that yields self-sustaining communities to have the

---

[152]Rathi, Shubhangi, 'Gandhian Philosophy of Sarvodaya and Its Principles', Bombay Sarvodaya Mandal & Gandhi Research Foundation, https://bit.ly/2G6Ibud. Accessed on 12 July 2022.
[153]Ibid.

freedom to choose the indigenous process by utilizing indigenous resources.

In addition to the decentralized system of governance, Gandhi assigned a greater role to the modern State on issues, such as land reforms and the use of armed forces for defence purposes.[154] The State should be morally motivated towards serving humanity selflessly and unconditionally without any vested interests. It is only then that a just and peaceful society can be visualized. This, in a way, meant that there should not be any difference between the purpose and the decision of the State and the inner voice of the individual. The State should serve every citizen of the nation, ensuring both materialistic and non-material welfare.

The source of the Gandhian paradigm, which is the powerful force of inner voice, has an immense ability to transform a rational consumer or investor into a more ethical and moral one. Guided by empathy and the law of non-possession, the ultimate aim of Gandhian economics is to build a society devoid of any concentration of power, competition, warfare and unrest.

Further, the twin models of trusteeship and economy of permanence advocate a spiritual enquiry and ethical value judgement as the fundamentals of Gandhian economics. Addressing the economic problem of scarcity and choice, the attributes of decentralization, self-sufficiency and self-reliance envisage that the individuals are satisfied with minimum consumption. In addition, a profound interconnectivity

[154]Pradhan, Ram Chandra, 'Gandhi's Hind Swaraj: A Summary and Centennial View', Bombay Sarvodaya Mandal & Gandhi Research Foundation, https://bit.ly/3NYmNsa. Accessed on 12 July 2022.

between the different aspects of non-violence, a subsequent balance in ecology and environment is created. The ethical responsibility is not just limited to socio-economic and political systems but also to the endeavours related to environmental and ecological sustainability.

The Gandhian ethics and morality manifested non-violence in humankind. Non-violence, truth and simplicity embodied the eternal values of life in his thoughts and actions. He advocated the sacredness of life that comprised trees, plants or even a cow, mainly the entire ecosystem around.[155] He argued that 'the greatness of a nation and its moral progress can be judged by the way its animals are treated.'[156] Gandhi was immensely inspired by Adolf Just's book, *Return to Nature*, which reinforces the fact that if a man desires to live a wholesome life, he will have to share his life with not only humans but all living beings, such as birds, animals, plants and the whole ecosystem.[157]

Nature has been considered as 'Mother Earth' by Gandhi. He believed that a man must return to nature what he takes from her. He rejected violence of any form towards animals or other living beings. Thus, he asserted the unity of life.[158] Gandhi propagated a way of living for humankind that sustains an ethical balance between the materialistic needs of humans and their responsibility towards ecology and environment. 'I believe in Advaita, I believe in the essential unity of man and,

---

[155]Jasper Margaret, C., *Animal Rights Law*, Oceana Publications, New York, 2002, p. vii.

[156]Gandhi, M.K., 'Is This Humanity?', *Young India*, Vol. 2, 1924–1926.

[157]Gandhi, M.K., Editorial in *Harijan*, 5 June 1937.

[158]Gandhi, M.K., 'Is This Humanity?', *Young India*, Vol. 2, 1924–1926.

for that matter, of all that lives. Therefore, I believe that if one man gains spiritually, the whole world gains with him and if one man fails, the whole world fails to that extent.'[159] The recent concept of deep ecology, by Naess, is highly inspired by the Gandhian belief of the oneness of all life forms.[160] This notion recognized the need to conserve all resources for the use of all species and not only human beings.

The Gandhian practice of observing silence was a phenomenal technique to communicate with the inner self and reach out to higher energy. This can also be considered as a novel method to conserve one's energy. The dissipative technology, as well as low-efficiency technology adopted by humans, have increased entropy (energy loss that is irreversible), conforming to the second law of thermodynamics, although human life or evolution is said to have violated the second law as a living being generates low entropy. To maintain the equilibrium, entropy has to be zero. The second law of thermodynamics advocates that entropy increases, leading to non-equilibrium and irreversibility. Human body exchanges energy from the external environment. However, the phenomenon of heat within the human body and the energy in the environment are in conflict with each other. Therefore, the system of the human body needs to be synchronized to maintain the thermodynamic equilibrium. In this context, by practising

---

[159]Neelakandan, Aravindan, 'The Charkha And The Cow', The Charkha and the Cow', Swarajya, 25 October 2016, https://bit.ly/3NThees. Accessed on 12 July 2022.

[160]Naess, Arne, 'The Shallow and the Deep, Long- Range Ecology Movement. A Summary,' *Inquiry*, Vol. 16, No. 1–4, 1973, pp. 95–100.

fasting and observing silence, the Gandhian philosophy successfully validates the law of the universe. through which thermodynamic equilibrium can be visualized.

'Gandhi's entire life functioned much like an ecosystem.'[161] His everyday life was constantly connected to the universe and was not bereft of ethics and morality. Humans need to connect themselves with nature and establish a symbiosis between their needs and the ecology. As per Gandhian philosophy, the continuity of life should be maintained by following the attributes of non-violence and absolute love. To maintain this continuity of life, humankind needs to pay enough respect to each other's works and perform daily activities considering the freedom of fellow humans. What emerges from nature should be returned to nature to keep the cycle of life functional—this also depicts the fundamentals of the theory of cradle-to-cradle system.

With emerging concerns of climate change, the energy discourse finds a crucial place for consideration. The developmental process since industrialization has been based on conventional energy system that has always worked in a centralized way. In fact, the preponderance of power on energy resources has been the key factor responsible for war and unrest. In this context, the Gandhian ideology of decentralization revolutionizes the energy regime, where small and independent communities based on consensus-based decision-making are self-sufficient in terms of energy sources.

Both energy conservation and energy efficiency are concepts related to the habits of individuals. The Gandhian

---

[161]Ibid. 24.

paradigm, which manifests an evolved consciousness within humankind, is highly sensitive to nature. Within this, every action and every thought emerge from a sense of responsibility and the individual is substantially motivated to preserve harmony with nature.

Gandhi revolutionized the way our society defined civil society, which has primarily emerged from historical events, such as the anti-colonial struggle, rise of western civilization and anti-globalization. Gandhian civil society has played a critical role in visualizing the Gandhian revolution not only in India but globally too. The Gandhian civil society has been extremely powerful in addressing issues at the global level, specifically the environmental issues. Several civil societies emerged in the US and UK, based on Gandhian principles during his lifetime.

Further, this decade of globalization also realized the fundamentals of Gandhian principles to be the best fit to cure all the disorders pertaining to environment, economy or world peace. The main features of Gandhian philosophy that influenced global civil society were the narratives against western modernity as propagated by Gandhi; they influenced several social movements.[162] Non-violent methods and satyagraha as a technique for dissent have been accepted widely. The Gandhian economic revolution has been embraced as a paradigm of development by global intellectuals as an alternate economic fundamental. In addition, the Gandhian notion of harmonizing humankind and nature has been deeply recognized by the world. On 15 June 2007, the

[162]https://bit.ly/3yGAGpd. Accessed on 14 July 2022.

United Nations General Assembly declared that 2 October would henceforth be observed as the International Day of Non-Violence.[163]

Based on Gandhi's novel thought of commons in the economic context, which found its profound connection with the notion of commons from an ecological sense, The Club of Rome and several global ecological movements were inspired.[164] The role of environmental movements undertaken by the global civil society based on Gandhian thoughts included opposition to big dams, strip mining, unregulated disposal of hazardous waste, the wanton destruction of animal and plant species, deforestation and several other endeavours to restore the notion of commons.[165]

All the subsequent environmental initiatives since the 1980s have been driven by Gandhian ecological paradigm. The Brandt Commission strongly emphasized that the prime objective of development is self-fulfilment and use of the nation's productive forces and human potential to achieve it.[166] In 1987, the Brundtland Commission report, titled *Our Common Future*, emphasized limits imposed by technology and social organizations as well as the ability of the biosphere to absorb the effects of human activities. In 1992, with the Rio Declaration on environment and development, the Convention on Biological Diversity was

---

[163]Ibid. 174.

[164]Lal, V., *Gandhi, Citizenship, and the Idea of a Good Civil Society,* Seva Mandir, https://bit.ly/3IDLuJb. Accessed on 14 July 2022.

[165] Ibid.

[166]Daptardar, Vaidehi, Dr, 'Gandhian Relevance to Environmental Sustainability', Bombay Sarvodaya Mandal & Gandhi Research Foundation, https://bit.ly/3z545La. Accessed on 15 July 2022.

formed to spread awareness on consumption patterns that had led to degradation of the environment.[167] Later, in 1997, the adoption of Kyoto Protocol made it legally binding to affect climate change. In 2006, *The Living Planet*, reported that the lifestyle followed in western societies disturbed the balance of planet earth.[168] In 2007–08, the *Human Development Report* on the theme 'Fighting Climate Change' emphasized, 'Climate change calls to question the enlightenment principle that human progress will make the future look better than past.'[169]

The awareness of consumption patterns that led to the degradation of the environment was unfolded with Gandhian economics of minimal consumption and non-material satisfaction that emerges from being able to distinguish desires from minimal wants. Later, the mention about the lifestyle, followed by the western societies, disturbing the balance of the planet Earth in the above mentioned initiatives once again highlight the relevance of the Gandhian paradigm, which rejects and condemns the idea of consumerism.

The Gandhian architecture has been extraordinarily vast to include all sociopolitical, economic and ecological facets of life. It is extremely incredible that Gandhi has been recognized for the immensely distinct aspects of his

[167]'Rio Declaration on Environment and Development', Convention on Biological Diversity, https://bit.ly/3z12QfY. Accessed on 14 July 2022.

[168]'What is the Kyoto Protocol?', United Nations Climate Change, https://bit.ly/2kIbtIW. Accessed on 14 July 2022.

[169]Daptardar, Vaidehi, Dr, 'Gandhian Relevance to Environmental Sustainability', Bombay Sarvodaya Mandal & Gandhi Research Foundation, https://bit.ly/3z545La. Accessed on 14 July 2022.

thoughts at the global level and mainly for his notions related to non-violence, economics, environment and ecology. In India, his presence has been felt mainly in the form of satyagraha as a mark of any protest or dissent. However, such protests are now not entirely guided by non-violence and instead, largely operated under political influence or agendas, with the true essence of selflessness and that of the soul force being lost.

While the world is revisiting Gandhian pathways and alternatives advocated by him, India is losing the essence of Gandhi. His insistence on clarity of means more than the ends was the underlying factor that structured all his movements as unique and distinct. If the means are compromised, then the ends will always be questionable. It is really disheartening to observe that today, Indians have been driven far away from their inner voice or soul force. Their pursuit for truth and self-sacrifice has been lost in the vicious cycle of materialistic development. We had already lost our inner voice the day we gave Gandhi's mortal existence a violent end. That unfortunate act of violence (means) certainly belittled the end of the world. The man who sacrificed his life for the pursuit of ethical and moral revolution was given a violent end. Gandhi even embraced his end non-violently, remembering the eternal truth or his inner voice. His ethically evolved inner voice is so profound that it will continue to guide humanity, establishing harmony between humankind and nature, leading us to the Gandhian paradigm.

Bibliography

Bondurant, Joan V., *Conquest of Violence: The Gandhian Philosophy of Conflict*, University of California Press, 1971.

Borman, William, *Gandhi and Non-Violence*, State University of New York Press, New York, 1986.

Brown, Judith M., *Gandhi: Prisoner of Hope*, Yale University Press, New Haven, 1991.

Camus, Albert, et al., *Resistance, Rebellion and Death*, Knopf, New York, 1960.

Chanshetti, Umakant, et la., 'Reduce, Reuse and Recycle: Sense of Responsibility in Mahatma Gandhi Global Village', *International Journal of Current Research*, Vol. 6, No. 9, 2014, pp. 8442–5.

Chatterjee, Margaret, *Gandhi's Religious Thought*, University of Notre Dame Press, 1983.

Dhavan, Gopinath, *The Political Philosophy of Mahatma Gandhi*, Popular Book Depot, Bombay, 1946.

Gandhi, M.K., *Democracy: Real and Deceptive*, R.K. Prabhu (ed.), Navajivan Publishing House, Ahmedabad, 1961.

Gandhi, M.K., *India of My Dreams*, Navajivan Publishing House, Ahmedabad, 1947.

Gandhi, M.K., *Mahatma and the Missionary: Selected Writings of Mohandas K. Gandhi,* Clifford Manshardt (ed.), Regnery Publishing, Chicago, 1949.

Gandhi, M.K., *Truth is God*, R.K. Prabhu (ed.), Navajivan Publishing House, Ahmedabad, 1955, p. 102.

Gandhi, M.K., *Socialism of My Conception*, Bharatiya Vidya Bhavan, Bombay, 1957.

Gandhi, M.K., *My Non-Violence,* Sailesh Kumar Bandopadhyaya (ed.), Navajivan Publishing House, Ahmedabad, 1960.

Girardet, Herbret (ed.), *Surviving the Century: Facing Climate Chaos and Other Global Challenges*, Routledge, 2008.

Guha, Ramachandra, *Gandhi Before India*, Vintage, New York, 2015.

Guha, Ramachandra, *Gandhi: The Years That Changed the World, 1914–1948*, Penguin Allen Lane, 2018.

Gupta, Dipankar, *From 'People' to 'Citizen': Democracy's Must Take Road*, Routledge, 2017.

Havel, Václav, *Summer Meditations*, Vintage Books, New York, 1993.

McDonough, William and Micheal Braungart, *Cradle to Cradle: Remaking the Way We Make Things*, North Point Press, 2010.

Mukherjee, Rudrangshu, *The Penguin Gandhi Reader*, Penguin Books, India, 1993.

Munasinghe, M. and McNeely Jeffrey (eds.), *Protected Area Economics and Policy: Linking Conservation and Sustainable Development*, World Bank, 1994, pp. 15–49.

Nanda, B.R., *Gandhi and His Critics*, Oxford University Press, New Delhi, 1985.

Parekh, Bhikhu C., *Colonialism, Tradition and Reform: An Analysis of Gandhi's Political Discourse*, Sage Publishing, New Delhi, 1989.

Parekh, B.C., *Gandhi's Political Philosophy: A Critical Examination*, Springer, 1989.

Parel, Anthony J., *Pax Gandhiana: The Political Philosophy of Mahatma Gandhi*, Oxford University Press, Oxford, 2016.

Pyarelal, *Mahatma Gandhi: The Last Phase*, Vol. II, Navajivan Publishing House, Ahmedabad, 1958.

Rao, Seshagiri K.L., *Mahatma Gandhi and Comparative Religion*, Motilal Banarsidass Publishers, Delhi, 1978.

Rudolph, Lloyd I. and Susanne Hoeber Rudolph, *The Modernity of Tradition: Political Development in India*, University of Chicago Press, Chicago, 1967.

Skidelsky, Robert, *Keynes: The Return of the Master*, Penguin, UK, 2010.

Terchek, Ronald J., *Gandhi: Struggling for Autonomy*, Rowman & Littlefield, 1998.

Young India, 4 December 1924.

Young India, 6 October 1921.

Young India, 26 November 1933.